THE CHILDREN'S ATLAS OF
Lost
Treasures

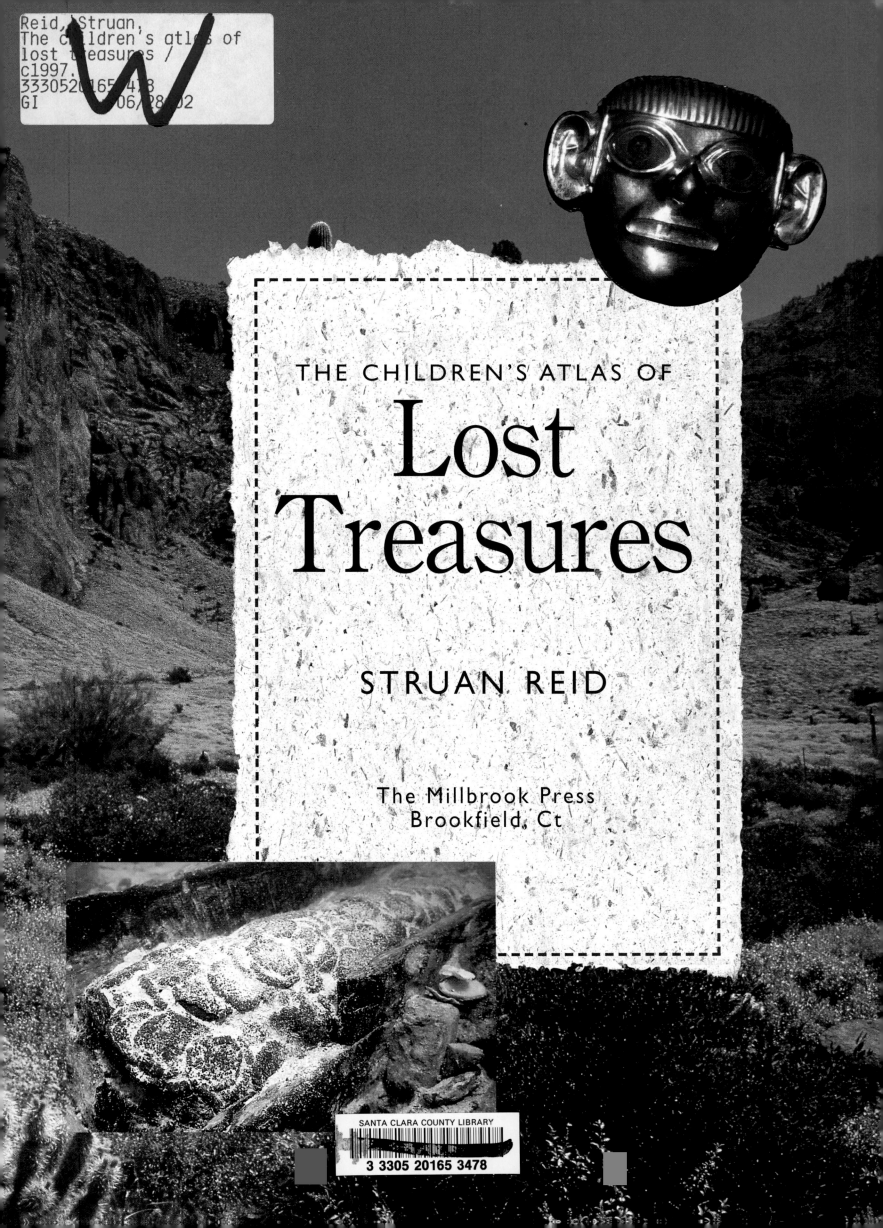

THE CHILDREN'S ATLAS OF

Lost Treasures

STRUAN REID

The Millbrook Press
Brookfield, Ct

A QUARTO CHILDREN'S BOOK

First published in the United States of America in 1997 by
Millbrook Press, Inc.
2 Old New Milford Road, Brookfield, Connecticut 06804

Library of Congress Cataloging-in-Publication Data

Reid, Struan.
 The children's atlas of lost treasures / Struan Reid. - - A
Millbrook Press Library ed.
   p.   cm.
 "A Quarto book."
 Includes bibliographical references and index.
 Summary: Surveys lost treasures around the world, including pirate
loot and treasures lost in wars and natural disasters.
  ISBN 0-7613-0219-0 (lib. bdg.). - - ISBN 0-7613-0240-9 (pbk.)
  1. Treasure-trove - - Juvenile literature.   [1. Buried treasure.]
I. Title.
G525.R3764   1997
910'.4'1 - -dc20

                                                          96-42453
                                                             CIP
                                                             AC

This book was designed and produced by
Quarto Children's Books Ltd,
The Fitzpatrick Building, 188 – 194 York Way, London N7 9QP

Creative Director Louise Jervis
Senior Art Editor Nigel Bradley
Editor Simon Beecroft
Project Editors Jean Coppendale and Honor Head
Designer Frances McKay
Picture Managers Pernilla Nissen and Su Alexander
Indexer Anita Reid
Consultant Dr Anne Millard

Illustrations by David Atkinson (maps), Peter Bates, Eric Bailey, Madeline David, (decoratives)
Keith Madison, Peter Massey, Ted Mc Craig/*Virgil Pomfret Agency*, Roger Stewart

Quarto would like to thank the following
for providing photograph and for granting permission to reproduce copyright material.
While every effort has been made to trace and acknowledge all copyright holders, we would like to apologize for any omissions.

(b = bottom, c *= center,* l *= left,* r *= right,* t *= top)*

Cover: Peter Newark's Historical Pictures; Title page: *tr* ET Archive, *bl* Planet Earth Pictures, background Trip / T. Mackie; *6bl* & *tl* AKG London, *br* ET Archive, *tr* Peter Clayton; *7tr* & *bl* ET Archive; *8b* ET Archive, *tl* & *tr* AKG London; *9t* Mansell Collection, *c* AKG London, BL Lesley & Roy Adkins; *br* Planet Earth Pictures; *10b* Peter Clayton; *11tl, c* & *b* Peter Clayton; *12bl* Peter Clayton, *br* & *cl* British Museum; *13br* AKG London, *c* Peter Clayton; *14bl* Peter Clayton; *tr* Mansell Collection; *15bl* & *cr* Peter Clayton; *16bl, br* & *cr* AKG London; *18bl* & *br* Peter Clayton; *c* ET Archive; *19br* & *tl* ET Archive; 20br & *tc* Peter Clayton; *21tl* Peter Clayton, *22bl, c* & *br* Peter Clayton; *23bl* & *t* ET Archive, *c* Peter Clayton; *24bl* Peter Clayton; *25bl* & *br* Peter Clayton, *b* Manchester Museum; *26b* & *tr* AKG London; *27t* China News Agency; *28t* & *bl* Peter Clayton; *29tl* British Museum, *br* ET Archive; *30br* ET Archive; *31tl* ET Archive, *bl* Frances McKay; *32bl* & *tr* ET Archive; *33br* ET Archive; *34bl* British Museum; *35t* & *b* AKG London; *36br* & *t* AKG London; *37b* AKG London, *c* Trip/B.Devine, *t* Mansell Collection; *38bl* Trip/A. Bloomfield, *br* Peter Clayton; *39tl* & *br* AKG London; *40bl* Peter Clayton, *c* British Museum; *41bl* British Museum; *42cl* Peter Clayton, *br* Hulton Getty Picture Collection; *cr* Trip / R. Panichelli, *tl* Peter Newark's Historical Pictures; *44bl* courtesy of Wartski, *c* & *tr* Novosti (London); *45br* ET Archive, *bl* Christie's Images, *tl* Novosti (London); *46b* Michael Nicholson; *47b* The Vasa Museum; *48b* Planet Earth Pictures; *49b* Michael Nicholson; *50br* J. Allan Cash Ltd; *51bl* & *tl* ET Archive; *52bl* & *tr* Mary Rose Trust, *tc* ET Archive; *53c* & *b* The Vasa Museum; *54cl* Planet Earth Pictures; *55bl, br* & *c* Planet Earth Pictures; *56t* Planet Earth Pictures, *b* Hulton Getty Picture Collection; *57tl, c* & *bl* Hulton Getty Picture Collection; *58b* ET Archive; *59tl* & *bl* Christie's Images, *br* ET Archive; *60b* ET Archive, *cl* Hulton Getty Collection; *61b* ET Archive, *tl* Hulton Getty Picture Collection; *62bl* Peter Clayton; *63bl* Hulton Getty Picture Collection, *tr* ET Archive; *64b* Peter Clayton, *c* Trip; *65b* AKG London, *tl* ET Archive; *66bl* & *t* ET Archive; *67bl, br* & *cl* ET Archive, *tl* Peter Newark's Historical Pictures; *68bl* Peter Clayton, t Peter Newark's Historical Pictures; *69bl* & br Visual Arts Library, *tl* ET Archive; *70bl* & *t* Novosti (London); *71t, c* & *b* Novosti (London); *72b* Continental Stamp Supplies, London; *73tl* & *br* ET Archive; *74bl* & *c* Hulton Getty Picture Collection; *75bl, br, c* & *tl* Hulton Getty Picture Collection; *76b* ET Archive; *77b* ET Archive, *t* AKG London; *78bl* J. Allan Cash; *79b* Peter Clayton; *80bl* Peter Newark's American Pictures, *c* South American Picture Library; *81br* ET Archive, *tl* South American Picture Library / Tony Morrison; *82bl* Hulton Getty Picture Collection, *br* Peter Newark's Historical Pictures; 83 *bl* Trip / R.Panichelli, *cr* Hulton Getty Picture Collection, *tl* ET Archive; *84bl* AKG London; *85b* ET Archive; *86b* ET Archive; *87br* & *tl* Peter Newark's Historical Pictures; *88bl* & *br* Peter Newark's Western Americana; *89bl* Trip / J. Dennis, *c* Northwind Pictures, tl Trip/ T. Mackie

Manufactured by Centre Media, London
Printed by Star Standard Industries (Pte) Ltd, Singapore

CONTENTS

SECRETS OF THE SOIL

FOR THOUSANDS of years, ever since people have had valuable possessions, they have guarded their wealth. So how do some treasures get lost?

▲ *The famous Lion Gate of Mycenae. It was built in about 1250 B.C. and formed the main entrance into the fortified city. Inside the gateway, German archeologist Heinrich Schliemann found spectacular gold treasures (page 16).*

Sometimes precious objects have been left in a hurry, dropped accidentally, or lost in a disaster. More often, they have been hidden or buried. In this book you will read about some spectacular discoveries of lost treasure from all over the world.

▶ *Bronze helmet found in the Sutton Hoo ship burial in Suffolk, England. It probably belonged to a king but his body was never found (page 16).*

◀ *Gold necklace found at the site of Troy (modern Hissarlik) in Turkey. It was part of the collection that went missing at the end of World War II (page 36).*

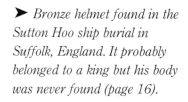

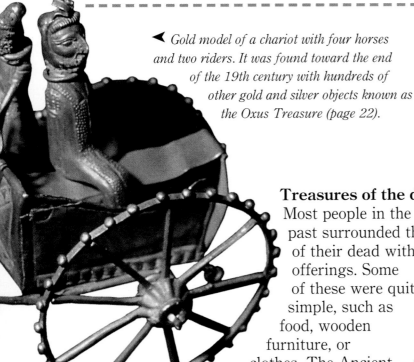

Gold model of a chariot with four horses and two riders. It was found toward the end of the 19th century with hundreds of other gold and silver objects known as the Oxus Treasure (page 22).

Treasures of the dead

Most people in the ancient past surrounded the remains of their dead with offerings. Some of these were quite simple, such as food, wooden furniture, or clothes. The Ancient Egyptians, Greeks, Etruscans, Chinese, and many other civilizations have furnished the tombs of their dead with precious objects. These treasures were never meant to be recovered but were left to ensure a comfortable life for the dead in the next world. Gradually these tombs and their contents were forgotten until they were discovered years later.

Abandoned treasures

In times of trouble, in war or revolution, or when natural disasters occur, people have been forced to abandon their homes quickly. Fearing looters, they hid their most valuable possessions in the hope of coming back to collect them once peace returned. But often something prevented them from recovering their property. Many treasures have been lost in natural disasters such as earthquakes, floods, and volcanic eruptions, or they have sunk to the bottom of the seas when a ship has been wrecked in a storm. Usually they were destroyed and lost for ever, but occasionally the cause of their loss has actually saved them. As in the city of Pompeii (page 38) buildings and objects can be preserved under a blanket of ash, while thick silt and mud on the sea-bed can seal objects in a virtual time capsule.

Stolen treasures

Pirates and robbers have often buried their stolen treasure in secret places to collect it at a later date. Again, for different reasons, they were sometimes unable to go back for their booty and the knowledge of its whereabouts died with them.

Gold model of a raft dating to about 1200, used during the El Dorado ceremony in South America. Many people went in search of the fabulous treasures of "The Golden One" (El Dorado) who is said to have thrown handfuls of gold and emeralds into a sacred lake (page 80). This model was one of the offerings.

Gold ornament of a panther's head found in the tomb of a warrior-priest in Peru in 1987. The tomb was full of gold treasures and jewelry (page 34).

LURE
OF GOLD

▲ *The Mask of Agamemnon found at Mycenae by Heinrich Schliemann. He believed he had uncovered the remains of the legendary Agamemnon, King of Mycenae and hero of the Trojan Wars.*

FOR THOUSANDS of years people have been fascinated by gold. It was probably one of the first metals to be discovered and has been used by many different cultures to make symbols of wealth and power and objects for religious worship. Gold has also attracted treasure-hunters for generations. Through the centuries, the lure of gold has drawn people to it like a magnet and many have even died in their pursuit of gold and other treasures.

THE ELGIN MARBLES

In 1816, British diplomat Lord Elgin brought a collection of sculptures from the Acropolis in Athens to London. Known as the Elgin Marbles, they are now on show in the British Museum. This panel shows riders in a religious ceremony.

Grave robbers

Robbing tombs is a profession as old as the tombs themselves. The Ancient Egyptians stopped building vast pyramids for their dead kings because the tombs were so frequently broken into and the contents looted. Instead they were buried in secret tombs hidden away in the Valley of the Kings. But even in this remote spot they found no refuge from the tomb robbers.

▲ *When people visited Egypt at the end of the 18th century, they were amazed at the beauty and enormous size of the sculptures they saw there. Many objects were shipped out of Egypt to museums throughout Europe.*

A 19th century engraving showing visitors among the ruins of Pompeii. Although the discoveries and excavations of the Roman city encouraged a growing interest in ancient remains, many of the objects discovered were quickly hidden away in private collections.

Graves in Italy, Greece and Russia were also looted in ancient times and the plundering continues today. Graves in Central and South America, Turkey, and Italy are still being broken into and the treasures inside sold to greedy collectors all over the world.

Early archeologists
The search for treasure also attracts another kind of dedicated professional: the archeologist. But archeology also began as a form of treasure-hunting. Early archeologists often destroyed as much as they saved in their search for gold and silver or beautiful works of art to add to their private collections.

A scientific study
Today all that has changed and archeology has become a careful, scientific study of all the remains of past human life, from the

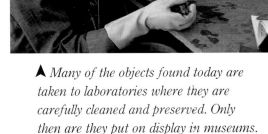

A Many of the objects found today are taken to laboratories where they are carefully cleaned and preserved. Only then are they put on display in museums.

great treasures of grand civilizations to the simplest domestic objects.

Scientific advances help archeologists and historians work out where to look for remains of the past, the probable age of the objects they find, what they are made of and also how best to preserve them. The development of aerial photography and, more recently, satellite photography has revealed traces of ancient sites that could not be seen from the ground. X-ray and infra-red photography can show the delicate patterns and designs on corroded metal objects. Carbon 14 (radio-carbon) dating is used to work out the age of organic remains such as fossils, bones, plants and shells This method can be used to date objects up to 50,000 years old.

A Photographs taken from the air often reveal a clear pattern of archeological remains and can show detail that cannot be seen from the ground.

A The invention of the aqualung and other equipment now enables archeologists to reach the wreckage of ships that have lain hidden beneath the sea for centuries.

OFFERINGS TO THE GODS

THROUGHOUT HISTORY many groups of people have believed that death is more than just the end of life. They believed in an afterlife in which the spirit lives on. The spirit had to be taken care of and provided with comforts similar to those the dead person enjoyed when alive. Most ancient societies therefore buried their dead with the things they believed they would need in the next world.

The sort of burial a person received depended on his or her position in society when alive. The poor and unimportant were usually given far less attention than the rich and famous. But the skeletons and objects found in all graves provide valuable information about the customs and beliefs of people in the past. However, it is not surprising that the more spectacular burials of royalty and the aristocracy have attracted far more attention than the others. Although many of these rich tombs were looted centuries ago, others remained undisturbed.

Royal burials

Perhaps the most famous royal tomb of all is that of the boy-king, Tutankhamun, who ruled Egypt for a short time in the 14th century B.C. His tomb, which contained the mummified body of the young pharaoh, was excavated in the 1920s. It revealed the incredible treasures that were buried with the Egyptian kings.

In many societies, important burials were covered with large mounds of stone or earth. The most spectacular of all are, of course, the Egyptian pyramids. Ancient Scythian tombs in Pazyryk, Siberia were covered with huge piles of stones. One of the most puzzling of these mound burials is the extremely rich burial of an entire Viking longship at Sutton Hoo in England. There was no sign of a body and the fabulous gold, enamel, and silver treasures buried inside suggest that the people believed in a mixture of pagan and Christian gods.

MAYAN TREASURE
p30-31

SIPAN TOMBS
p32-33

▲ *More than two hundred pieces of jewelry were found in Tutankhamun's tomb. Many were made of gold inlaid with colored glass and precious stones.*

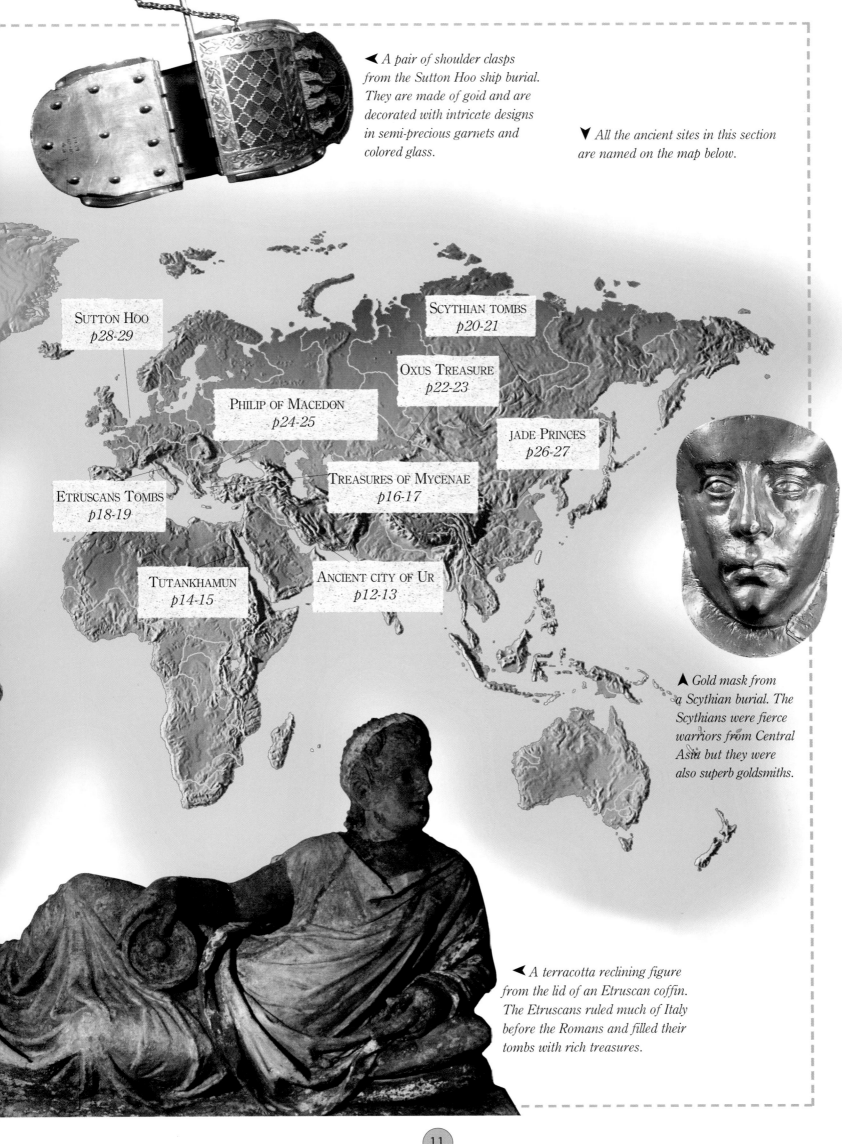

◄ *A pair of shoulder clasps from the Sutton Hoo ship burial. They are made of gold and are decorated with intricate designs in semi-precious garnets and colored glass.*

▼ *All the ancient sites in this section are named on the map below.*

SCYTHIAN TOMBS
p20-21

SUTTON HOO
p28-29

OXUS TREASURE
p22-23

PHILIP OF MACEDON
p24-25

JADE PRINCES
p26-27

TREASURES OF MYCENAE
p16-17

ETRUSCANS TOMBS
p18-19

TUTANKHAMUN
p14-15

ANCIENT CITY OF UR
p12-13

▲ *Gold mask from a Scythian burial. The Scythians were fierce warriors from Central Asia but they were also superb goldsmiths.*

◄ *A terracotta reclining figure from the lid of an Etruscan coffin. The Etruscans ruled much of Italy before the Romans and filled their tombs with rich treasures.*

ANCIENT CITY OF UR

THE ANCIENT CITY OF UR (in present-day Iraq) was once one of the most powerful cities in the Middle East. It was mentioned in the Bible as the birthplace of the prophet Abraham, but for thousands of years it had been lost and forgotten. Then, in 1854, the site of the city was identified from the remains of a huge man-made structure known as a ziggurat.

Discovering the rulers of Ur

In 1922 one of the greatest archeologists of the 20th century, Leonard Woolley, started his excavations at Ur. He worked for five years before he finally found what he was looking for – the graves of the rulers of Ur. Over the next twelve years, Woolley found sixteen royal tombs near the ziggurat. They dated to about 2500 B.C. Most of the tombs had been looted but incredibly two remained untouched.

One was full of gold and silver treasures and fantastic jewelry. In another tomb, named the Great Death Pit, he found a spectacular gold and silver helmet, together with the remains of three lyres, one of gold and two of silver.

▲ *Leonard Woolley took great care with the delicate fragments of objects he found. Here, he uncovers a small pottery figure.*

THE BULL'S HEAD LYRE

A number of musical instruments were found at Ur, including this lyre (a type of harp) with a golden bull's head. When the instruments were discovered the wooden parts had rotted away leaving only the pieces of metal and stone inlay lying in place in the soil. With care and patience, many of the instruments have been rebuilt.

◄ *One of the many objects discovered is the Royal Standard of Ur. Made of pink stone, shell, and a decorative blue stone called lapis-lazuli, it was probably the sound box of a wooden harp.*

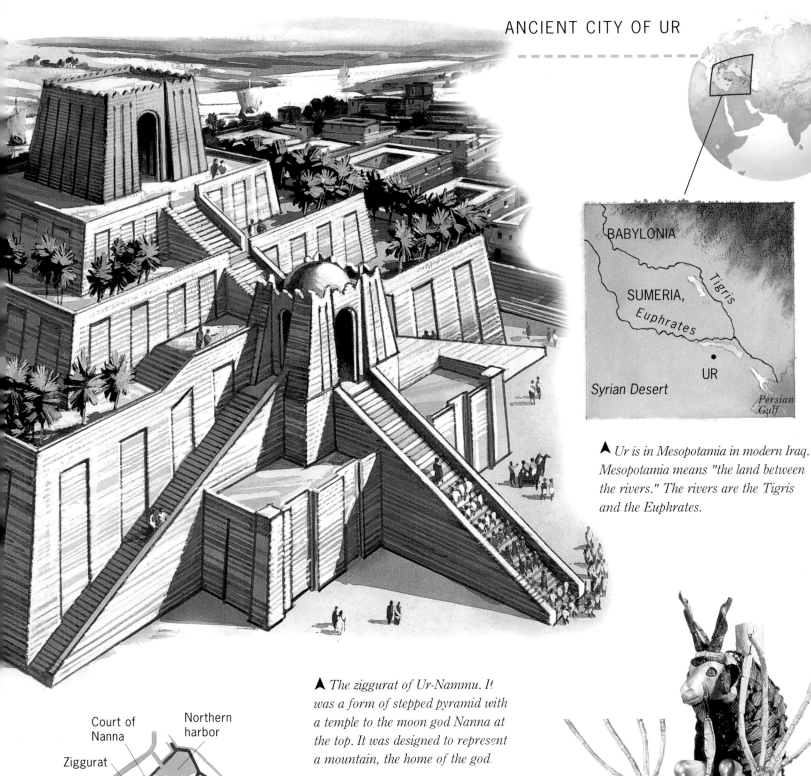

▲ Ur is in Mesopotamia in modern Iraq. Mesopotamia means "the land between the rivers." The rivers are the Tigris and the Euphrates.

▲ The ziggurat of Ur-Nammu. It was a form of stepped pyramid with a temple to the moon god Nanna at the top. It was designed to represent a mountain, the home of the god.

▼ A gaming board made from hundreds of pieces of colored stone. The wooden framework had rotted away and had to be recarved. The stone fragments were carefully cleaned and then remounted.

▲ Layout of the ancient city of Ur. The ziggurat is near the center and the palaces and cemetaries are around it. The ziggurat was the focal point of the entire city.

➤ A figure of a ram with its forefeet in a tree in gold and lapis lazuli. Blue lapis lazuli was highly prized in ancient times. It was mined in northern Afghanistan and exported to Mesopotamia.

TREASURES OF THE BOY-KING

ONE OF THE MOST AMAZING discoveries ever made was in 1922 on the western bank of the Nile River in Egypt. Here, after eight years of searching, two British archeologists, Howard Carter and his rich patron the Earl of Carnarvon, finally came across the tomb of the young pharaoh Tutankhamun (reigned 1347-1337 B.C.).

Carter and Carnarvon had begun their search in 1914, but they had found nothing. In a final attempt, Carter began digging near the tomb of a later pharaoh, Ramses VI. Almost immediately the workmen found the top of a staircase that led under the ground. They cleared the steps and at the bottom found a door. The unbroken seal on the door gave two pieces of information: that this was the entrance to a royal tomb and that no one had opened the door for more than 3,000 years. On the other side was an inner door. Carter broke a small hole in the plaster of the door and peered through.

He was looking into a chamber piled high with beautiful objects and furniture. Many of them carried Tutankhamun's name inscribed in hieroglyphs. Among them was his golden throne set with semi-precious stones. Behind this was another chamber with a huge gold shrine that filled the entire room. The shrine contained a series of coffins. Inside the innermost coffin, made of solid gold, lay the well-preserved body of the young pharaoh, Tutankhamun.

▲ *Howard Carter gently brushing away the rotting linen shroud which covered the face of the second coffin.*

► *The entrance to the treasury, beyond the burial chamber, was guarded by the jackal-headed god, Anubis. Behind him is the large gilded shrine which contained the embalmed internal organs of the young pharaoh.*

► *One of the thrones of Tutankhamun. It is made of wood and covered with gold and silver.*

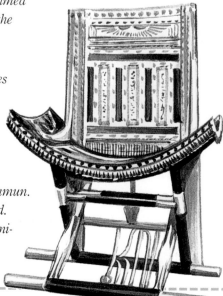

◄ *The magnificent gold mask of Tutankhamun. It shows the king as Osiris, ruler of the dead. The gold is inlaid with colored glass and semi-precious stones of red carnelian and blue lapis lazuli.*

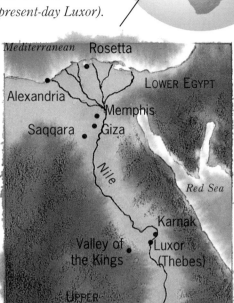

▼ *Many pharaohs were buried in the Valley of the Kings near Thebes (present-day Luxor).*

Mediterranean   Rosetta

Alexandria

LOWER EGYPT

Memphis

Saqqara   Giza

Nile

Red Sea

Karnak

Valley of   Luxor
the Kings   (Thebes)

UPPER
EGYPT

Aswan

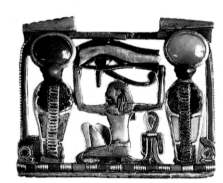

▲ *Gold pectoral pendant set with colored glass and semi-precious stones. It was designed to be hung from a chain round the neck.*

▲ *A view of the Valley of the Kings where Tutankhamun's magnificent tomb was found.*

"THE CURSE OF TUTANKHAMUN"

Some time after the discovery of Tutankhamun's tomb, a story spread that the pharaoh had laid a curse on anyone who disturbed his grave. When Lord Carnarvon died suddenly in 1923, people believed that the pharaoh was taking his revenge. In fact, there was no such curse and Lord Carnarvon died from the results of infections after he had been bitten by a mosquito.

▶ *Diagram showing the arrangement of Tutankhamun's tomb. In the center is the main burial chamber with the mummy of the king in its stone sarcophagus (coffin) surrounded by its shrines.*

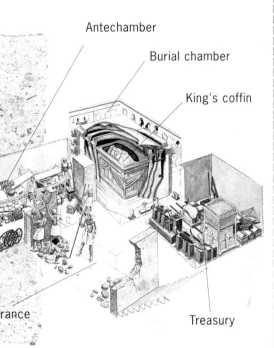

Antechamber

Burial chamber

King's coffin

Entrance

Treasury

TREASURE OF MYCENAE

FOR ABOUT FIVE HUNDRED years from 1600 B.C., Mycenae was the most important city in the Greek world. It was also the city of the legendary King Agamemnon who had fought the Trojans. In 468 B.C. Mycenae was destroyed by invading armies from the neighbouring city of Argos. But the location of Mycenae was well known because its magnificent ruined walls remained standing down the centuries.

In 1876, a rich German businessman called Heinrich Schliemann, who was fascinated by Homer's tales of Greek heroes and the siege of Troy (see page 37), began excavating the ruins. First, he uncovered the massive Lion Gate, the entrance to the royal palace at Mycenae. Inside, his workmen cleared a circle of upright stone slabs. They were carved with figures of soldiers fighting on foot and in chariots, as they would have done in the Trojan Wars. Then, the workmen found a series of shafts that led underground.

A dazzling collection

Climbing down into the shafts, Schliemann and his assistants found the most dazzling collection of ancient gold, silver and bronze treasures that had ever been discovered. There were cups, goblets, and jewelry, and bronze helmets and swords. The shafts also contained skeletons, including three of men wearing heavy gold masks. The skulls of two of them had crumbled away, but under one mask the skull was still intact. Schliemann thought this might be Agamemnon himself, but he was wrong for later scientific tests on the skeletons proved that the skulls belonged to a much earlier period.

▲ *Heinrich Schliemann (1822-1890), made a huge fortune in business and retired at 41. He spent the rest of his life trying to prove the facts behind Homer's account of the Trojan Wars.*

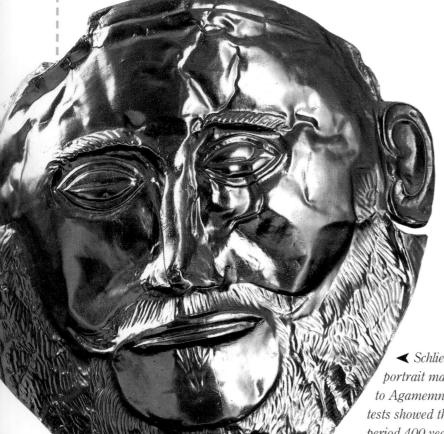

◄ *Schliemann thought this portrait mask belonged to Agamemnon. But scientific tests showed that it dated to a period 400 years earlier.*

▲ *The huge stone Lion Gate at Mycenae was built in about 1250 B.C. It is named after the two heraldic lions that decorate the top. They are shown with their front paws resting on a column.*

▼ *Mycenae was the most important Greek city between about 1600 and 1110 B.C.*

Troy
GREECE   *Aegean Sea*
Athens
Argos
Sparta   Mycenae
Crete   Thera
Mediterranean Sea

ROYAL BURIALS AT MYCENAE

There were two types of royal burial at Mycenae. The earlier, simpler type is known as a shaft grave and consists of a deep pit dug into the ground. The shaft grave could be more than 39 feet (12 meters) deep and usually contained several bodies, perhaps from the same family. By about 1500 B.C., shaft graves were replaced by huge underground stone chambers called *tholos* or beehive tombs. The most famous of these is the so-called Treasury of Atreus.

▼ *This large beehive-shaped chamber is known as a* throlos *tomb. This is a cross-section of one, named by Schliemann the Treasury of Atreus after another king of Mycenae.*

The burial chamber was over 42 feet (13 meters) high

▲ *Schliemann and his team working in one of the shaft graves inside the Lion Gate. Here, they are lifting out a golden diadem. Above stands one of the stone slabs carved with battle scenes.*

The dome interior was originally covered in bronze ornaments

ETRUSCAN TOMBS OF ITALY

PEOPLE CALLED THE ETRUSCANS ruled much of northern and central Italy from about 700-400 B.C. many years before the rise of the Roman Empire. But because their civilization was destroyed by the Romans and their language is still not properly understood, little is known about them. However, clues to their way of life gathered from their tombs show them to be an artistic and fun-loving people. Wealthy Etruscans built elaborate underground tombs which they furnished like their own homes.

City of tombs

Thousands of these tomb-houses were built next to each other with streets running between them. The walls inside the chambers were brightly painted with lively scenes of daily life. The bodies of the dead were put in enormous stone coffins. Around the coffins were placed their portraits carved in stone and terracotta.

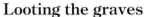

▲ *The Etruscans were excellent goldsmiths and many beautiful pieces of jewelry have been found in their tombs.*

With the dead were also placed many of their personal treasures and household furnishings to accompany them in the afterlife. Items of gold, silver, bronze, marble, and terracotta were packed into jars and boxes and placed inside the tombs. There were wooden tables, beds made of bronze, and golden goblets as well as beautiful Greek vases. There were also silver mirrors, bronze statuettes of warriors, and decorative incense burners.

▲ *An Etruscan gold brooch in the form of a griffin and a sea serpent.*

Looting the graves

For hundreds of years the Etruscans and their rich civilization lay buried and forgotten. Their tombs, unlike many from ancient times, remained untouched. Then, in the early 18th century people became interested in the Etruscans.

In 1728, the necropolis (burial ground) and town of Volterra were excavated, and the site workers were amazed when they found beautiful gold and silver objects inside. Word spread and many other Etruscan sites were opened and stripped bare of their treasures. The looting continued well into the 20th century and many superb pieces of jewelry, bronzes and pottery were sold and scattered all over Europe. The skeletons of the dead and many of the beautiful frescoes were damaged in the process.

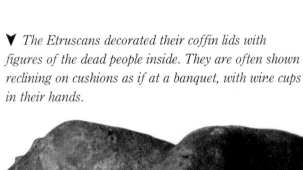

▼ *The Etruscans decorated their coffin lids with figures of the dead people inside. They are often shown reclining on cushions as if at a banquet, with wine cups in their hands.*

▲ At the peak of their power, the Etruscans ruled an area of Italy stretching from the Po River in the north, to Naples in the south.

◄ The Etruscans decorated the walls of their tombs with paintings showing scenes of daily life. As their writing is not fully understood, these paintings have provided archeologists with much information about their daily life. From looking at these tomb paintings, it is clear that the Etruscans enjoyed life to the full. In this painting found in the Tomb of Leopards, Tarquinia, men and women are shown at a special banquet being served food and entertained by musicians.

INSIDE THE TOMBS

Thousands of Etruscan tombs have been found and it would take far too long to excavate them all. As many have already been looted, archeologists look into a tomb first to find out whether it should be excavated or not. A small hole is drilled through the roof of the tomb and then a miniature camera with a flashlight is lowered through the hole. The camera takes a series of photographs to show what is inside the tomb.

TOMBS OF THE WARRIOR NOMADS

IN 1929, SOME RUSSIAN archeologists went to investigate a group of burial mounds in the Pazyryk Valley in the far east of Russia. The mounds were marked by huge piles of stones and turned out to be the burial places of chieftains of the Scythian people. The Scythians were fierce nomadic tribesmen who lived on the steppes of central Asia from the ninth to the fourth centuries B.C. The Pazyryk Valley lies in part of Siberia and the archeologists had to chip their way through the frozen earth beneath piles of stones and then use boiling water to melt their way into the tombs below. It was obvious from the condition of the tombs that they had been looted by robbers, probably soon after the burial. In their rush to get out with their booty, the

▲ *Gold death mask of a Scythian queen. Many beautiful ornaments were found in their tombs.*

robbers left holes in the roofs of the tombs. Water seeped into them, flooding everything inside and then froze solid. The tombs had been turned into giant deep freezers, preserving the remains inside.

Objects made from materials that normally rot away, such as textiles and leather, were almost as bright and fresh as when they were first buried 2,400 years earlier.

In one tomb were the bodies of two men and a woman laid out in huge coffins carved from tree-trunks. The arms, legs, and backs of the men were tattooed with animal patterns while the woman had a long black pigtail and was dressed in a fur cloak and felt boots. On the floor of one tomb was a thick Persian carpet (the oldest carpet ever discovered) and the walls were covered with embroidered felt hangings.

TATTOOED BODIES

The bodies of the men in one of the Pazyryk tombs were covered with elaborate tattoos. They were made by pricking the skin and then rubbing the marks with black ink. There were a number of strange designs on the arms, legs, and backs: winged creatures with lions' tails, wild asses and mountain goats, and deer with birds' beaks.

▲ *This gold vase was probably made by a Greek craftsman working for a Scythian chieftain. This view shows two Scythians playing dice. It also shows the sort of clothes the men wore — wool tunics and trousers and long leather boots.*

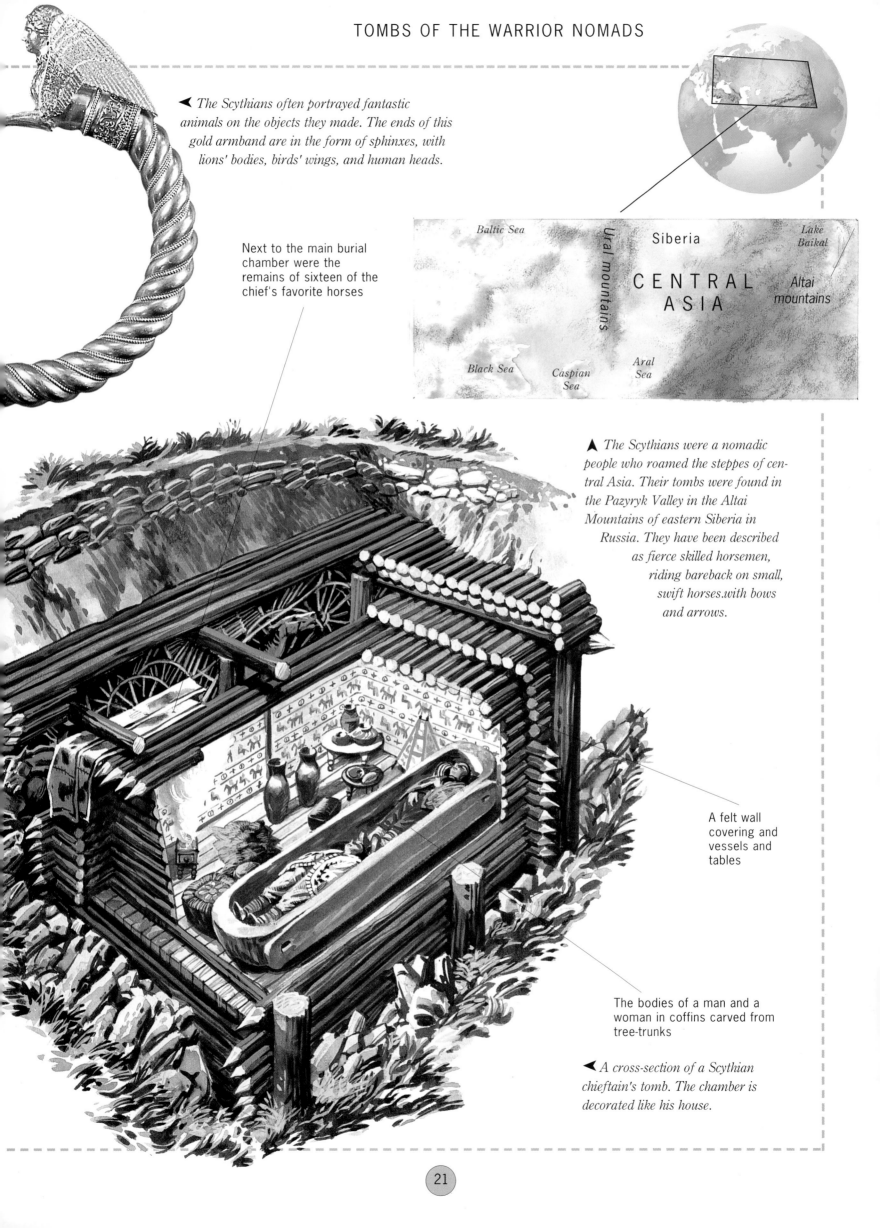

◄ *The Scythians often portrayed fantastic animals on the objects they made. The ends of this gold armband are in the form of sphinxes, with lions' bodies, birds' wings, and human heads.*

Next to the main burial chamber were the remains of sixteen of the chief's favorite horses

Baltic Sea

Ural mountains

Siberia

Lake Baikal

CENTRAL ASIA

Altai mountains

Black Sea

Caspian Sea

Aral Sea

▲ *The Scythians were a nomadic people who roamed the steppes of central Asia. Their tombs were found in the Pazyryk Valley in the Altai Mountains of eastern Siberia in Russia. They have been described as fierce skilled horsemen, riding bareback on small, swift horses.with bows and arrows.*

A felt wall covering and vessels and tables

The bodies of a man and a woman in coffins carved from tree-trunks

◄ *A cross-section of a Scythian chieftain's tomb. The chamber is decorated like his house.*

MYSTERY OF THE OXUS TREASURE

IN 1880, A BRITISH officer based in Afghanistan called Francis Burton chanced upon an incredible discovery. He had been asked for help by the servant of three merchants who had been kidnapped while traveling from Afghanistan to Rawalpindi in India. The merchants and their servant had been set upon by a group of bandits and carried off into the mountains. The servant managed to escape and had gone in search of help. Burton and two assistants set off to catch up with the bandits. They had only traveled a short distance when they found the bandits and their hostages hiding in a cave for the night. As Burton crept into the cave, an extraordinary sight met his eyes. The thieves had obviously had a violent argument over the fate of the merchants and their goods. Four of them had been wounded in a fight and lay stretched out on the floor of the cave. The merchants were huddled in a corner, terrified that they might be killed, and their goods were scattered all around them. Burton could hardly believe his eyes as he saw golden bowls, bracelets, cups, and necklaces glinting in the dim light.

▲ This model of a chariot drawn by four horses shows the great skill of the Persian goldsmiths. The two figures are wearing Median clothes, a style worn by the Medes, one of the peoples conquered by the Persians.

Retrieving the treasure

Burton released the merchants and let them take some of the treasure. The thieves made off with the rest. Later, Burton sent out a message that unless all the treasure was returned to the merchants the bandits would be hunted down and punished. Nearly all the gold pieces were secretly returned. There were massive gold armlets decorated with winged griffins, hundreds of gold coins, and a silver statue of a Persian king. Many of the pieces included depictions of people and animals. Where they came from is uncertain, but the merchants claimed that they had been dug up three years earlier beside the Oxus River between Afghanistan and Russia. Once the merchants reached the trading city of Rawalpindi they sold the items separately. Over the following years pieces would appear in local bazaars (markets) and many of them were bought by England and are on display in the British Museum in London. Others were probably melted down or sold elsewhere.

◄ Figure of a Persian king carrying a flower, cut out of a sheet of gold. It shows him wearing a long, richly embroidered tunic with boots, an elaborate hairstyle and beard, with a crown on his head.

► Gold dish with a line of lions around the edge, probably used for ceremonies.

➤ *The Oxus Treasure is named after the river Oxus (now the Amu-Darya) which is in Uzbekistan and flows between Afghanistan and Russia.*

▲ *With its high mountains and deep valleys, Afghanistan has always been a difficult region for foreign powers to control. In the 19th century, bandits had their hideouts in caves and crevices and would swoop down on travelers.*

▲ *Gold armbands like this were given as official presents by the Persian kings. This one would originally have been inlaid with semi-precious stones.*

▲ *The tomb of Cyrus the Great is unique as most Persian kings were buried in rock-cut tombs.*

CYRUS THE GREAT

One of the greatest Persian rulers was Cyrus II 'the Great' (reigned 559-529 B.C.). He was the founder of the Persian Empire. His tomb still stands at the site of his capital city at Parsargadae in Iran. It is a stone building in the shape of a small house.

PHILIP OF MACEDON

PEOPLE HAD KNOWN for many years about the huge mound of earth near the village of Vergina in Macedonia, Greece but it had never properly been investigated. Then, in 1977, a Greek archeologist named Manolis Andronikos began an excavation. Deep under the mound, a large stone tomb was uncovered and the archeologists saw that the door was untouched. Slowly levering the massive stone door open, Andronikos stepped inside and found that the entire tomb was undisturbed.

Exquisite treasures

There were two chambers inside containing exquisite gold and silver treasures. There was a beautiful gold bow case decorated with battle scenes, a bronze shield cover, an iron helmet, and a sponge which was still soft to the touch. More amazing, though, were two large marble boxes, each containing golden caskets. Inside these were the bones and ashes of two people. Nothing was found in the tomb to tell us who the two people were, but it was clear from the treasures that they were members of a royal family. Today, many archeologists believe that one of the caskets contained the remains of King Philip II of Macedon, the father of Alexander the Great, who reigned in the mid-fourth century B.C. The other probably contained the remains of his wife Cleopatra. A number of small ivory heads were found and one looked like portraits of Philip on his coins.

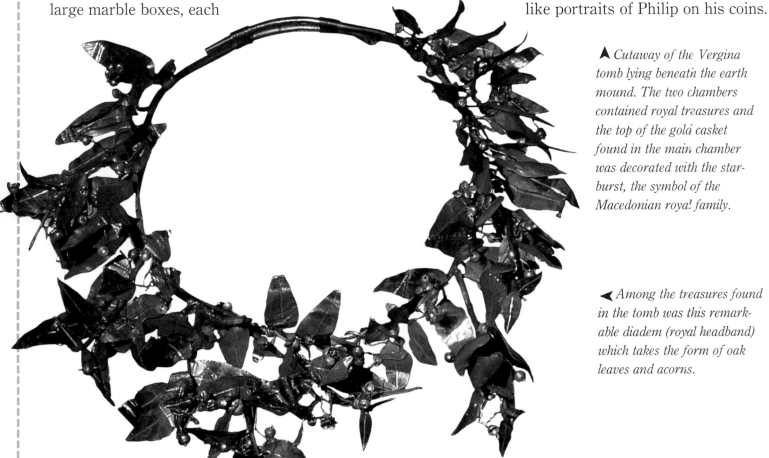

▲ *Cutaway of the Vergina tomb lying beneath the earth mound. The two chambers contained royal treasures and the top of the gold casket found in the main chamber was decorated with the star-burst, the symbol of the Macedonian royal family.*

◄ *Among the treasures found in the tomb was this remark-able diadem (royal headband) which takes the form of oak leaves and acorns.*

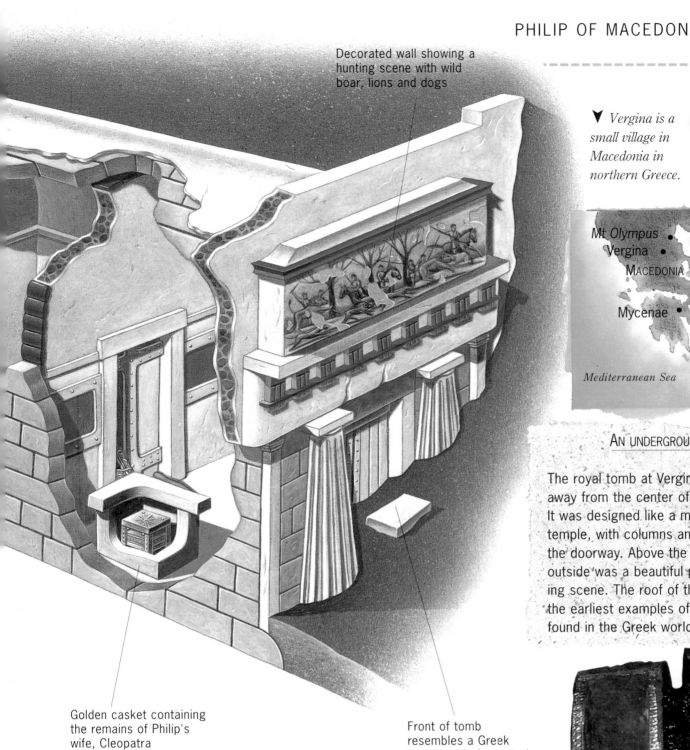

Decorated wall showing a hunting scene with wild boar, lions and dogs

Golden casket containing the remains of Philip's wife, Cleopatra

Front of tomb resembles a Greek temple with decorated columns

▼ *Vergina is a small village in Macedonia in northern Greece.*

Mt Olympus
Vergina
MACEDONIA
Aegean Sea
Mycenae
Athens
Mediterranean Sea
CRETE

AN UNDERGROUND PALACE

The royal tomb at Vergina was found far away from the center of the earth mound. It was designed like a miniature palace or temple, with columns and a portico round the doorway. Above the door on the outside was a beautiful painting of a hunting scene. The roof of the tomb is one of the earliest examples of a true vault ever found in the Greek world.

THE FACE OF PHILIP

1 The bones in one of the caskets belonged to those of a man of about forty years old. Philip was forty-six when he died in 336 B.C. A remarkable experiment was carried out by the British Museum to reconstruct the face of the man buried in the gold casket.
2 and **3** The fragments of his skull were stuck together and a wax cast was made of the head, with skin color, false hair, and beard.
4 The skull showed an injury to the right eye and Philip is known to have lost an eye in battle.

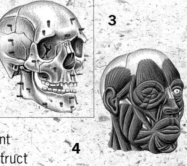

▲ *This iron breastplate is decorated with bands of gold and gold studs in the form of a lion's head on the front.*

ROYAL PRINCES

IN 202 B.C. A DYNASTY of emperors called the Han emerged as rulers of China and they were to reign for more than four hundred years. In 135 B.C. the Emperor Wu Ti appointed his brother Liu Sheng as governor of the Changshan region near Beijing. Liu Sheng and his wife ruled the province ruthlessly for more than twenty years until his death in 113 B.C. His wife Dou Wan died about ten years later.

The prince and princess were buried in tombs cut deep into the rocky hillsides near the town of Mancheng. There they remained for 2,000 years until June 1968 when soldiers came across a small hole that led deep underground. Climbing through the hole they found themselves in an enormous underground chamber and as they shone their torches round the dark walls the light caught the gleam of many gold and silver objects. The inscriptions on these objects were later to identify their owner as Prince Liu Sheng. Some time later, on a nearby hillside, the incredulous soldiers found the tomb belonging to Dou Wan.

In two side passages in Liu Sheng's tomb archeologists found six carriages and the skeletons of sixteen horses and eleven dogs. Hundreds of beautiful pots and statuettes were laid out in rows on the floors of the main chambers of both tombs. There were bronze swords and bowls inlaid with gold and silver, as well as lamps and incense burners.

Among the thousands of objects perhaps the most amazing discovery was what looked like piles of small jade plaques. On closer examination they turned out to be the burial suits of the prince and princess and the most complete examples ever found. Although the bodies of Liu Sheng and his wife had rotted away their magnificent burial suits had survived.

Lacquered coffins
They were made of thousands of small pieces of cut and polished jade. Each piece was linked to the next by gold wire. Dressed in their jade suits, the prince and princess were placed in lacquered coffins with their heads resting on bronze cushions inlaid with gold.

▲ *The jade burial suit of Princess Dou Wan, its head resting on a bronze and jade pillow. The Chinese believed that jade, a hard green stone, could prevent the body decaying. The suit is made of 2,160 pieces drilled in the corners and linked together with gold wire. Only members of the imperial family were allowed to use gold wire.*

◄ *An ornate vase found in the tomb of Prince Liu Sheng. It is made of bronze decorated with gold and the sides are covered with an elaborate design of intertwined dragons.*

► *The central chamber of the tomb of Liu Sheng. It was carved from solid rock. More than 2,800 objects, including gold, silver, and bronze items, were found in the tombs. The jade suits have been restored and, along with the other objects, are now in the Beijing Palace Museum, China.*

▼ *The tombs were found near Mancheng 90 miles (150 kilometers) southwest of Beijing.*

Great Wall
Beijing
Mancheng
Hwang (Yellow River)
Changshan region
Yangtze
Yellow Sea

► *Each of the jade suits was made in twelve separate sections which were fitted together round the body and then sewn with gold wire. Archeologists have estimated that each suit would have taken a craftsman more than ten years to make. The jade plaques were carefully matched for color and then polished on the outer surface.*

Liu Sheng's suit was in twelve parts

The suit is sewn with 2lb 7oz (1.1kg) of gold wire

The suit is 6ft 2in (1.88m) long

Tomb of Princess Dou Wan

Chamber containing body

Chamber containing body

Tomb of Prince Liu Sheng

ROCK-CUT TOMBS

The tombs of the prince and princeess were cut out of solid rock. Thousands of workmen had excavated more than 64,000 tons of rock to make the chambers.

Each tomb consisted of an entrance gallery with two long side chambers.

At the end of the gallery lay a huge antechamber and beyond this the burial chamber itself. When the prince and princess were buried, the mouths of their tombs were blocked with huge stones. Then molten iron was poured over the entrances to seal them and save them from robbers.

SHIP BURIAL AT SUTTON HOO

THE LAND around the site of Sutton Hoo in Suffolk, England was owned by a farmer called Mrs Edith Pretty. She had often wondered what lay beneath the group of earth mounds in one of her fields. Rumors had been circulating for generations that a fabulous treasure had been buried somewhere beneath them. But who built the mounds, and when?

▲ *One of the many treasures found in the ship was this purse lid. It was originally made of bone or ivory and decorated with gold panels set with garnets and colored glass.*

First clues

In 1938 Mrs Pretty asked local archeologists to investigate. Excavations were started on some of the smaller mounds. Only a few objects were found, such as fragments of pottery and human bones. These gave important information because the bones indicated that the mounds formed a large burial ground while the pottery gave a date of about A.D. 600. Encouraged by these discoveries, the archeologists resumed their excavations the following year, working on the largest mound.

Stunning discoveries

Digging deep into the soil, they began to uncover what were clearly the remains of a large boat. There were no timbers but long lines of rusty nails and dark marks in the soil that showed where the timbers had once been. The archeologists revealed the outline of a boat 89 feet (27 meters) long. After some weeks they came across the outline of a chamber that had been placed in the center of the boat. There, lying in the soil, were the most amazing treasures. There were magnificent pieces of heavy gold jewelry set with garnets and colored glass, beautiful silver dishes, bowls and spoons, the gold and garnet fittings to a sword, and the gold and bronze decoration of a shield. There was a royal scepter of stone and bronze and a golden purse containing thirty-seven gold coins.

This spectacular discovery was made just before the outbreak of World War II. Mrs Pretty donated the treasures to the nation but some weeks later they all had to be buried once again, this time in a tunnel deep beneath the streets of London to protect them from bombing raids. Five years later, at the end of the war, the magnificent treasures were finally put on display in the British Museum.

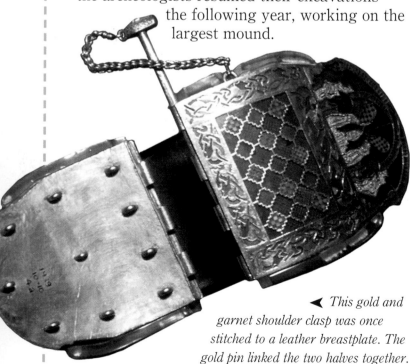

◄ *This gold and garnet shoulder clasp was once stitched to a leather breastplate. The gold pin linked the two halves together.*

WHO WAS BURIED AT SUTTON HOO?

Even though this was a burial, no body has ever been found. Either it was cremated and the ashes absorbed into the soil, or for some reason it was buried in another place. Whatever the case, the great richness of the treasures indicate a royal burial and the evidence points to a powerful king of East Anglia called Raedwald who died in about A.D. 625. He was a member of the Wuffinga dynasty, or 'wolf people'.

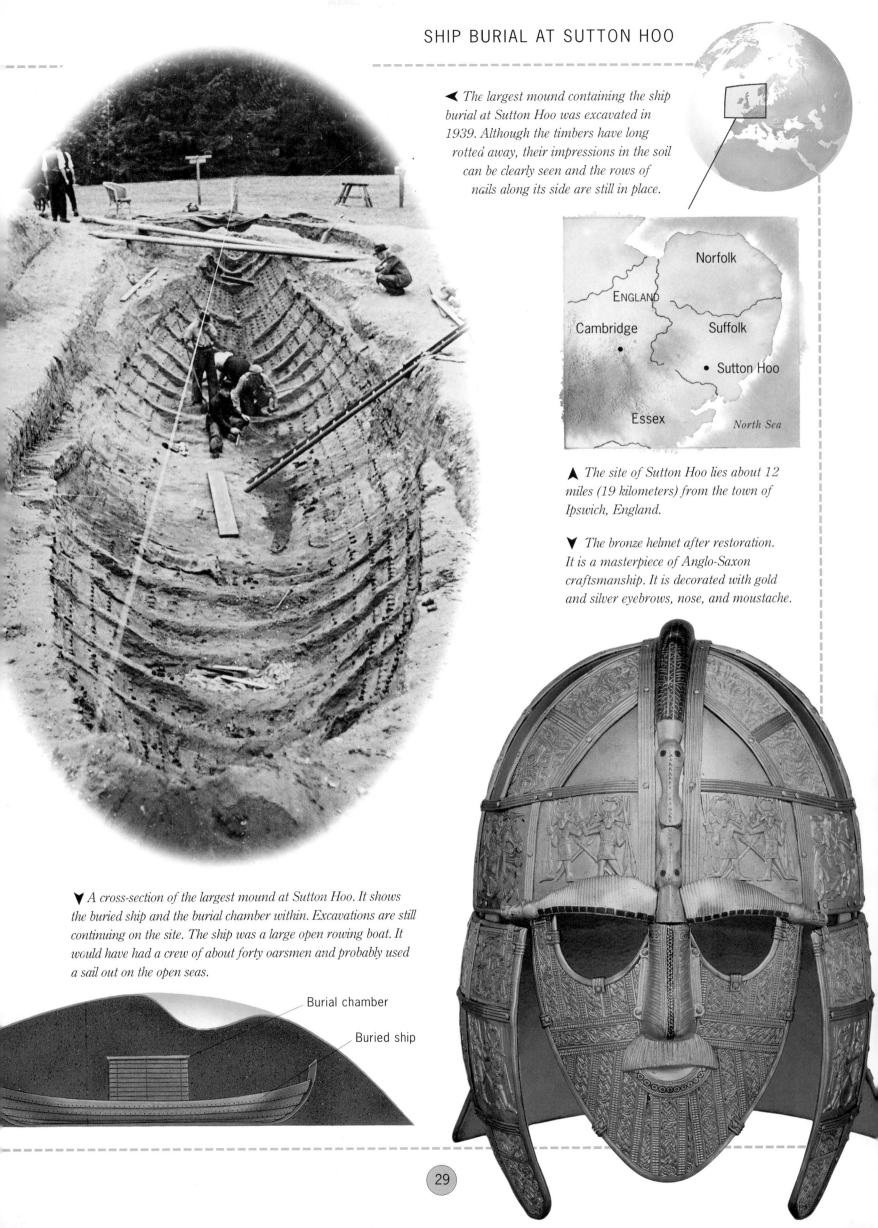

◀ The largest mound containing the ship burial at Sutton Hoo was excavated in 1939. Although the timbers have long rotted away, their impressions in the soil can be clearly seen and the rows of nails along its side are still in place.

▲ The site of Sutton Hoo lies about 12 miles (19 kilometers) from the town of Ipswich, England.

▼ The bronze helmet after restoration. It is a masterpiece of Anglo-Saxon craftsmanship. It is decorated with gold and silver eyebrows, nose, and moustache.

▼ A cross-section of the largest mound at Sutton Hoo. It shows the buried ship and the burial chamber within. Excavations are still continuing on the site. The ship was a large open rowing boat. It would have had a crew of about forty oarsmen and probably used a sail out on the open seas.

Burial chamber

Buried ship

CHICHEN ITZA AND THE MAYA

FOR THOUSANDS OF YEARS the Maya had one of the most advanced civilizations in the Americas. They were skilled farmers and used irrigation canals to bring water to their fields. They built splendid cities with beautiful stone palaces and stepped temple-pyramids, wide streets, and open plazas. Roads ran from one city to another and were used for large religious processions. The Maya civilization reached its peak between the years A.D. 200 and 900. In about 987 the more warlike Toltecs from the region near modern Mexico City invaded the Maya lands and took over their cities, ruling the area for nearly two hundred years until 1180.

One of the main Maya cities is Chichen Itza, built in the flat, dry plain of the Yucatan Peninsula. People always knew it was there but it remained unexplored until the first excavations were carried out in 1875. One of the most important places in the city was a huge well, known as the Cenote of Sacrifice. This is a large pool of water surrounded by deep cliff walls. It was a place of pilgrimage for both the Maya and the Toltecs (people from northern Mexico) who threw precious objects of gold, jade, copper, and pottery into the water as offerings to their gods.

In 1904-1907, a U.S. diplomat and treasure-hunter, E.H. Thompson, recovered a small number of precious objects from the well. In 1962 a second exploration of the well was sponsored by the National Geographic Society. Chemicals were used to clear the silt in the well and then divers were sent down. They recovered more than six thousand objects, including copper, jade, and gold items and the bones of forty-two humans sacrificed to the gods.

▲ *The Castillo of Chichen Itza. This 73 feet (22.25 meters) high stepped pyramid was built in the center of the city's main plaza with other important buildings placed around it. A temple stood at the top of the pyramid.*

▲ *Gold frog pendant. This was one of the many offerings to the gods thrown into the Well of Sacrifice.*

WRITING WITH SYMBOLS

The Maya were expert scientists, mathematicians, and astronomers who developed a complex system of writing using symbols called glyphs. It was the only writing of Central America which could be used to form full sentences and write stories. Each glyph had its own meaning and a sentence could be formed by placing several glyphs together. This stone slab, called a *stela*, is carved with glyphic writing. It comes from the Maya city of Tikal in Guatemala. Some glyphs list historical and political events.

Each block stands for a name, a date or a place.

The symbols were carved in pairs and read from left to right

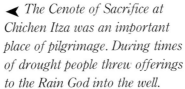

▲ *The Maya civilization flourished between A.D. 200 and 900 in part of what is now Guatemala and Mexico.*

BALL GAMES

The Maya played a ball game called pok-a-tok. The players had to hit a large rubber ball through a stone ring placed high up on a wall. They could use only their elbows, forearms, hips or knees. The game was played in long, thin courts surrounded by walls from where large crowds could watch.

◄ *The Cenote of Sacrifice at Chichen Itza was an important place of pilgrimage. During times of drought people threw offerings to the Rain God into the well.*

▼ *One of the jade tablets carved with human figures recovered from the Cenote of Sacrifice. The Maya valued jade more highly than gold.*

ROYAL TOMBS OF SIPAN

Between the years A.D. 100-800, the Moche civilization flourished along the northern coast of Peru. The people were warriors, farmers, and fishermen. They were also skilled water engineers and used an elaborate system of canals to irrigate their dry land. Until quite recently, little was known about these people who lived in Peru many years before the Incas. Remains of the Moche civilization consisted mainly of mudbrick platform tombs and pyramids and beautiful pottery which gave clues about the daily and religious life of the people. Until the 1980s, most of the known Moche tombs had been looted

Then in February 1987, robbers were digging on one of the small mudbrick pyramids when they broke into an unlooted burial chamber. There were gold ornaments in the shape of large peanuts, gold necklaces and bracelets, a golden

▲ *This Moche ornament is made of gold. It is thought to represent a panther's head.*

flute, and a solid gold head with enormous eyes of lapis lazuli and silver. The police were called and local archeologists started work.

Later, an even more spectacular discovery was made when archeologists inside the pyramid found the skeleton of a man with both feet amputated. Then not far below they came across a large wooden coffin and inside were the remains of another man. His body was surrounded by wonderful treasures, including feather headdresses, embroidered clothes, and beautiful gold and silver jewelry.

▼ *This gold funerary mask was one of the beautiful gold objects rescued by police from looters. Another mask, matching this, was sold for U.S. $60,000.*

LORD OF SIPAN

The man in the main coffin is now known as the Lord of Sipan after the valley where he was found. He was believed to have been about thirty-five years old when he died and may have been a warrior-priest. His coffin was surrounded by five others containing the bodies of two men and three women.

▶ *Reconstruction of the mudbrick pyramid containing the tomb of the Lord of Sipan.*

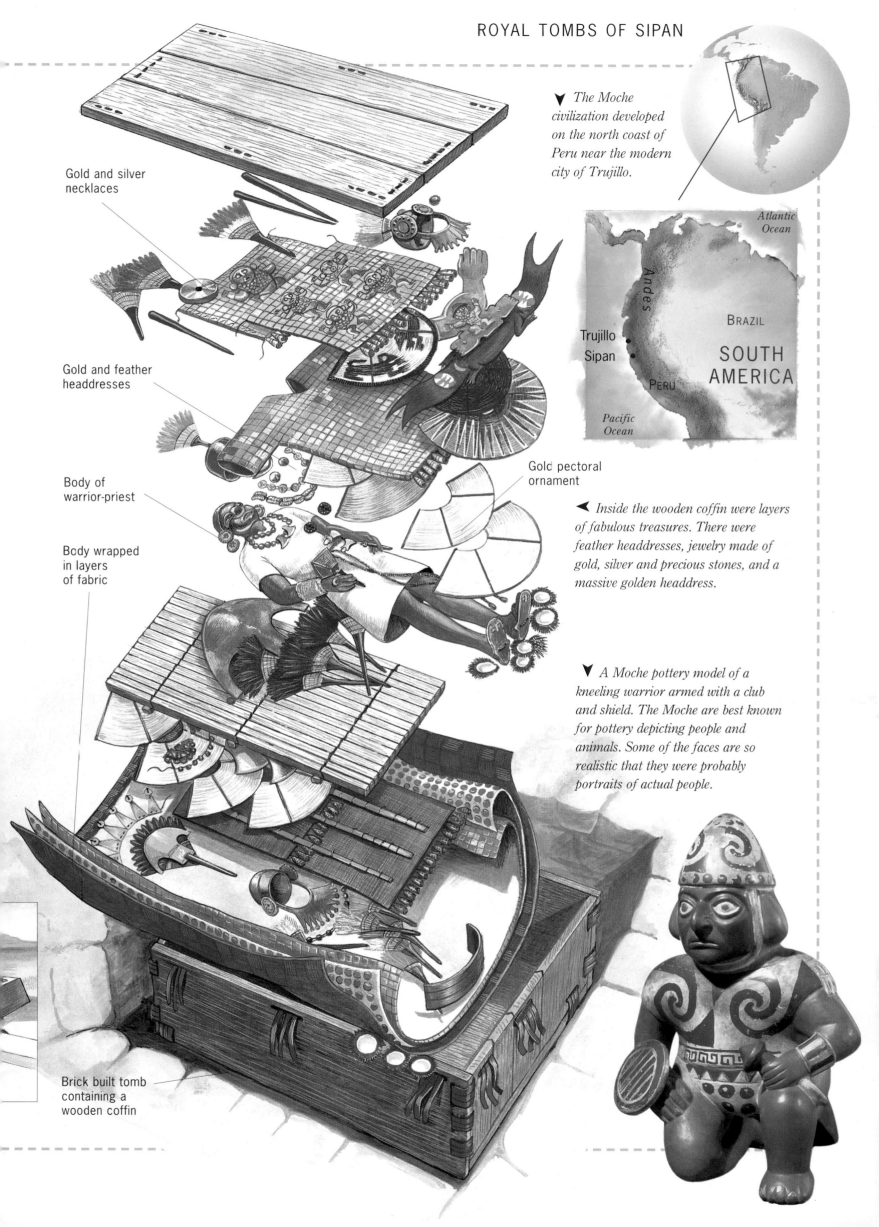

Gold and silver
necklaces

Gold and feather
headdresses

Body of
warrior-priest

Body wrapped
in layers
of fabric

Gold pectoral
ornament

Brick built tomb
containing a
wooden coffin

▼ *The Moche
civilization developed
on the north coast of
Peru near the modern
city of Trujillo.*

Atlantic
Ocean

Andes

Trujillo

Sipan

PERU

Pacific
Ocean

BRAZIL

SOUTH
AMERICA

◄ *Inside the wooden coffin were layers
of fabulous treasures. There were
feather headdresses, jewelry made of
gold, silver and precious stones, and a
massive golden headdress.*

▼ *A Moche pottery model of a
kneeling warrior armed with a club
and shield. The Moche are best known
for pottery depicting people and
animals. Some of the faces are so
realistic that they were probably
portraits of actual people.*

WAR, PIRACY, AND DISASTERS

A LOT OF TREASURE has been lost when cities were destroyed in wars. Buildings have collapsed, burying the treasure beneath tons of rubble before looting soldiers could get their hands on it. Other treasures have been just as suddenly lost, covered up, or swept away by natural disasters such as a flood or a volcanic eruption.

Hidden treasure

Many hoards of treasure have been deliberately hidden. As German tribes began to attack the Roman Empire from the end of the fourth century, many families hid or buried their valuables. Both rich and poor left their homes taking only the barest necessities with them. Often they were never able to reclaim their treasures and they remained hidden for centuries. About 600 such hoards have been found in France alone and there must be many more still to be discovered.

Later, in the mid-16th century, when the English King Henry VIII was confiscating church property – a time known as the Dissolution of the Monasteries – monks and nuns hid the treasures of their convents and monasteries. At the end of the 18th century in France, many family treasures were hidden during the time of the French Revolution.

◄ *Valuable possessions are often hidden in times of trouble. This enormous Roman silver dish was found buried in a field in Suffolk, England with many other silver objects.*

▼ *The sites in this section are named on the map below.*

MARY DEAR
p42-43

Pirate plunder

Pirates' booty has been concealed in all sorts of places. Piracy flourished from the 16th to the 19th centuries when ships sailed between Europe, the East, and the Americas, laden with gold and silver bullion, jewels, and other precious cargoes. Many hundreds of these ships were attacked by pirates. The leaders often died violently before they had revealed the secret locations of their stolen wealth.

◄ *Treasures can be suddenly lost in the destruction of a city. This oil painting of 1813 shows the Roman historian Pliny watching the eruption of Mount Vesuvius in A.D. 79.*

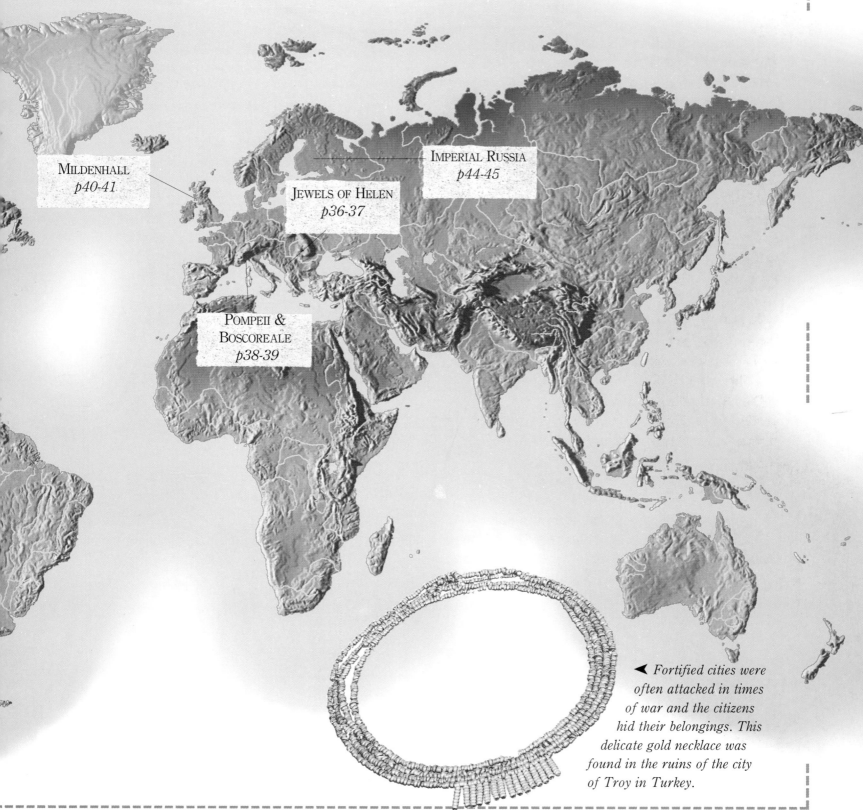

◄ *Fortified cities were often attacked in times of war and the citizens hid their belongings. This delicate gold necklace was found in the ruins of the city of Troy in Turkey.*

TROY AND THE JEWELS OF HELEN

In 1870, HEINRICH SCHLIEMANN, a rich German businessman fascinated by the stories of Homer (see pages 16-17), began excavating a huge earth mound at a place called Hissarlik in Turkey. Schliemann wanted to find the lost city of Troy and to prove that Homer's stories were true.

He hired a team of 160 workmen to dig up the mound. They continued for four years, removing hundreds of tons of earth and, in the process, doing terrible damage. In his determination to find Homer's Troy, Schliemann encouraged his workmen to smash their way through the remains of other ancient buildings to reach the level where he thought Homer's city must have been and much valuable evidence was lost for ever.

The glint of metal

In June 1873, Schliemann and his wife Sophia were watching the excavation when he suddenly noticed the glint of metal in the earth. Schliemann climbed into the deep trench and started digging out the metal objects himself. He unearthed a copper cauldron and plate, a jug and two cups of solid gold, copper spears, and beautiful ceremonial knives made of silver. Then he lifted out silver jars packed with the most amazing gold jewelry. Schliemann was sure that he had found the personal treasure of Priam, the ancient King of Troy.

The Schliemanns discovered about 8,700 metal objects. There were gold and silver jars and goblets, bronze weapons, and a stunning collection of gold necklaces, diadems, bracelets, and buttons, which he named the "Jewels of Helen." But Schliemann had been carried away in his excitement and was completely wrong. What they had in fact found was a collection of gold and silver from the Early Bronze Age of about 2000 B.C., a period at least 1,000 years before King Priam and the Trojan Wars.

➤ *A gold hairpin with a square top decorated with a row of tiny gold goblets.*

➤ *Sophia Schliemann wearing the so-called "Jewels of Helen." They believed the runaway queen of Sparta had once worn this spectacular jewelery.*

▲ *A gold earring with a basket-shaped top from which hang five pendants. Each pendant hangs from a chain.*

➤ *Inside the main citadel of Troy. Although Schliemann's excavations destroyed valuable evidence, it has been discovered that many successive cities had been built on the same site. Excavations on the site continue to this day.*

◄ The site of Troy (Hissarlik) is in Turkey, near the Dardanelles and looks across the Aegean Sea towards Greece.

HOMER THE STORYTELLER

Little is known about Homer. Historians believe that he was an Ionian Greek who lived in the ninth or eighth century B.C. He composed the two poems the *Iliad* and the *Odyssey* which were probably first written down a few centuries later. The *Iliad* tells the story of the last days of the ten-year siege of Troy by the ancient Greeks.

▲ Bust of the blind poet, Homer. This is a Roman copy of a Greek original.

► According to legend, the people of Troy were tricked into allowing a gift of a huge wooden horse into their city. Greek soldiers were hidden inside. They crept out under cover of night and opened the city gates to the rest of the Greek army waiting ouside.

► One of the gold necklaces found at Troy. It is made up of hundreds of pieces of decorated gold linked together on thread. It has been reconstructed with a great deal of skill and patience.

POMPEII AND BOSCOREALE

THE ROMAN TOWNS of Pompeii and Herculaneum in southern Italy were flourishing in the first century A.D. Pompeii had large open squares, public baths, a town hall, and a 5,000 seat theatre. Both towns played an important part in the life and prosperity of the Roman empire.

All of this came to a sudden end on August 24, A.D. 79, when Mount Vesuvius, a volcano which lay behind the two towns, erupted. Pompeii was covered in a blanket of ash nearly 13 feet (4 meters) deep, while Herculaneum was engulfed in a wave of boiling mud. Everyone in the towns, and for miles around, was smothered to death.

They lay entombed for more than 1,500 years until Pompeii was rediscovered by chance in 1594. Herculaneum was rediscovered in 1709. But proper excavations did not start at Pompeii until 1860 when careful records were taken of all the discoveries and the buildings were protected.

The disaster of A.D. 79 also wiped out the small village of Boscoreale, lying near the foot of Mount Vesuvius. Nearly 2,000 years later in 1894, a local man named Vincenzo de Prisco uncovered the remains of a large Roman villa. He later found the skeleton of the owner's wife still lying on her bronze bed, adorned with gold and jewelry. Close by lay the skeleton of a servant. Some months later, in 1895, they uncovered the doorway into a cellar. On the floor inside was the skeleton of a man crouching over his personal fortune – a gold chain, gold earrings, bracelets, and hundreds of coins. Inside the room was a huge pile of silver vessels – bowls, cups, basins, ewers, and dishes – all had become blackened with age. The Boscoreale Treasure was later sold in Paris, France and forty-one of the best pieces are now in the Louvre Museum.

▲ *A view of Herculaneum which was destroyed at the same time as Pompeii. Its remains were discovered in 1709.*

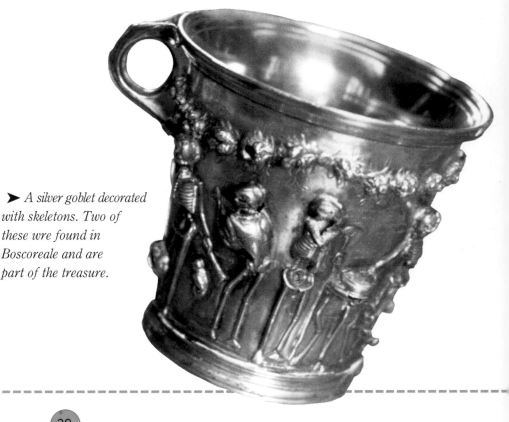

➤ *A silver goblet decorated with skeletons. Two of these wre found in Boscoreale and are part of the treasure.*

▼ *Herculaneum, Pompeii, and the area, including Boscoreale, were destroyed in a volcanic eruption of Mount Vesuvius in A.D. 79. The volcano has erupted ten further times since.*

◀ *A painting of the eruption of Mount Vesuvius. In the foreground is the Roman historian Pliny who wrote about the disaster.*

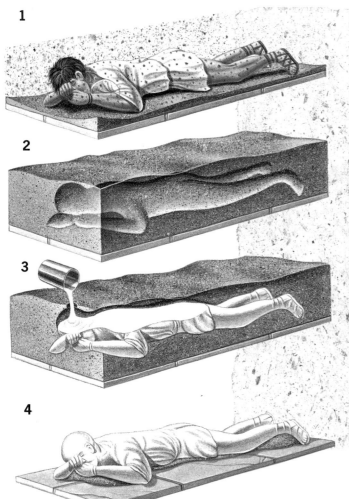

1

2

3

4

RAISING THE DEAD

In 1860, Italian archeologist Giuseppe Fiorelli devised a method of recovering the corpses of the people and animals killed during the eruption of Mount Vesuvius.

1 Body covered by fallen ashes
2 Body decomposes leaving a hollow shape in the now hardened ashes
3 Fiorelli poured liquid plaster into holes
4 When the plaster set the exact shape of the body could be excavated

▼ *A loaf of bread found in the ash of Pompeii. It was ready to be eaten when the disaster happened and it turned to stone. Nearly 2,000 years later it can be seen in the Naples Museum in Italy.*

TREASURES OF MILDENHALL

WHILE PLOUGHING some fields near the town of Mildenhall in Suffolk, England in 1942, a farmworker noticed some metal objects poking up through the soil. He and the owner of the land set about digging up the earth. They found thirty-four pieces of tableware – dishes, goblets, spoons, bowls, and ladles – most of them beautifully decorated. What they had discovered was the most spectacular hoard of Roman silver ever found in England. The landowner decided to hide the treasure away in his house where it remained for the next four years. It was not until 1946, one year after the end of World War II, that the farmer decided to tell the authorities. By then it was too late, for the British law of treasure trove states that any find of gold or silver must be reported straight away. If he had done so, the farmer would have been rewarded with the value of the treasure – perhaps by as much as $750,000. Instead he received a token payment of $1,500.

The treasure was handed over to the British Museum in London where, after cleaning, its full beauty was revealed. Experts dated the Mildenhall Treasure to about A.D. 370. The wealth of the treasure suggests that it must have belonged to an important Roman official and some scholars think the owner may have been a Christian Roman general called Lupicinus.

At this time the eastern parts of Britain, including Suffolk, were being attacked by Saxons from across the North Sea. The treasure may have been buried in a hurry during one of these Saxon raids to be collected later but its owner never came back for it.

▲ *This round silver dish with decorated lid was part of the treasure.*

▶ *The Mildenhall Treasure, discovered in 1942 by a farmer ploughing a field, comprised in total thirty-four pieces of mostly fourth century Roman silverware.*

◀ *This silver spoon is one of many found at Mildenhall. Some of the spoons were decorated with Christian symbols whereas the rest of the treasure was adorned with pagan (non-Christian) scenes.*

North Sea

SCANDANAVIA

Schleswig

ENGLAND

Baltic Sea

GERMANY

Mildenhall

▲ *The treasure was found near the market town of Mildenhall in England. It was hidden by a wealthy Roman family who feared invasion by Saxon pirates from Schleswig in Germany.*

▼ *The centerpiece of the treasure is the Great Dish which measures 1.6 feet (half a metre) in diameter and weighs over 17 pounds (8 kg).*

RAIDERS FROM ACROSS THE SEA

The Saxons were a tribe who came from the area of modern Schleswig in Germany and along the Baltic coast. The Roman empire in the West was beginning to collapse in the late fourth and early fifth centuries A.D. and the Saxons quickly spread through northern Germany. Saxon pirates also began attacking the coasts of Britain and France at this time.

TREASURE OF THE *MARY DEAR*

COCOS ISLAND is a volcanic rock that sticks up in the Pacific Ocean near Panama. The most famous story associated with Cocos Island is that of the *Mary Dear*. In 1820 a British sailor called Captain Thompson agreed to transport a group of rich Spaniards from Peru back to Spain on his ship called the *Mary Dear*. His passengers brought as many of their possessions as they could. These included chests overflowing with gold and silver plates, bags of gold coins and precious stones, and rare books. There were also solid silver candlesticks and other rich relics snatched from churches and cathedrals.

Death on the high seas

The agreement the passengers made with Thompson was that he would take them to Spain in return for a large sum of money. But Thompson and his crew were completely overwhelmed by the amazing riches they had seen and decided to murder the passengers. They were all slaughtered and the *Mary Dear* sailed with the treasure to Cocos Island.

Once there, Thompson and his crew buried it in the forests and left. In Mexico they were arrested by the Spanish and imprisoned. But Thompson bribed his guards and managed to escape. He returned to Cocos Island and retrieved some of the stolen treasure, but most of it was still thought to be buried when he died. Many people believe the treasure is still hidden there waiting to be discovered.

▲ *Gold coins are part of the treasure buried on the Cocos Islands.*

▼ *A late 18th century engraving showing a view of Cocos Island in the Pacific Ocean. The island is covered in thick forest and was a favorite hideout for pirates because it was within striking distance of the rich Spanish colonies in Central and South America.*

▼ *This scene shows a pirate of the late 17th century looking on as his crew bury stolen treasure.*

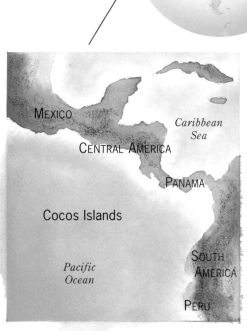

▲ *Cocos Island in the Pacific Ocean is 500 miles (805 kilometers) from Panama. It covers an area of about 20 square miles (50 square kilometers).*

▼ *A view of the beach at Chatham Bay, Cocos Island. It is just inland from here that the treasure of the* Mary Dear *is supposed to have been buried.*

➤ *Cocos Island: among the famous pirates who are supposed to have buried their treasure on the island are William Dampier and Edward Davis.*

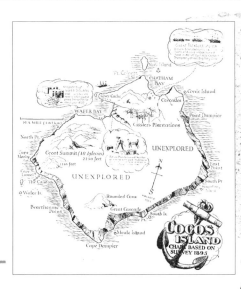

TREASURE HUNTERS OF COCOS ISLAND

There have been many treasure-hunting expeditions to Cocos Island. One of the first was led by August Gissler in the 1890s. He found some gold coins but spent a fortune of his own looking for treasure. One of the most recent expeditions to recover hidden treasure was started in 1975 and was called The Industrial and General Marketing Company. To date they have not found anything.

TREASURES OF IMPERIAL RUSSIA

▲ *Nicholas II (1868-1918), was one of the richest men in the world.*

On the night of July 16, 1918, in the cellar of a modest house in Yekaterinburg, Siberia, Tsar Nicholas II of Russia, his wife, daughters, and son were executed by Russian revolutionaries. Their bodies were quickly burned and the remains thrown into an old mineshaft. Nicholas's family, the Romanovs, had ruled Russia for more than 300 years, from 1613, and over that period they had amassed a huge fortune from mines producing gold, silver, precious stones, and coal.

The tsar and his family owned objects of great value and beauty. Many of these were created by Peter Carl Fabergé, goldsmith and court jeweler, who produced some of the most exquisite objects of gold, enamel, and precious stones.

▲ *Photograph of the Russian Imperial family in 1918 on the roof of a house in Tobolsk. They were kept prisoners here until they were transferred to Yekaterinburg where they were assassinated.*

When Nicholas was forced to abdicate in 1917 during the Russian Revolution, the crown jewels and many of the treasures of the imperial family were seized by the new Communist masters of Russia. Some of the gold, silver, and paintings were sold to finance the revolution but many of the other pieces are now kept in the Kremlin Museum in Moscow, the Hermitage in St Petersburg, and museums in Europe and North America.

After his death, rumors spread that Tsar Nicholas must have hidden away many more fabulous treasures in secret locations in Russia and throughout Europe. He did have gold and money deposited in banks outside Russia but only a small amount has ever been found and this was in a bank in Germany.

▲ *Peter Carl Fabergé (1846-1920) was one of the most brilliant jewelers of his day.*

JEWELER TO THE TSARS

Peter Carl Fabergé was born in 1846 in St Petersburg. His father was a jeweler and he inherited the family business. His workshop was famous for the beautiful pieces which he made for Russian and European royalty in the shapes of flowers, animals, and, especially, Easter eggs. He went into exile in 1917 and died three years later in Lausanne, Switzerland.

▼ ➤ *Some of the ornate objects created by Fabergé. Some of the larger eggs, opened up to reveal surprises such as miniature golden coaches.*

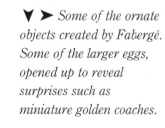

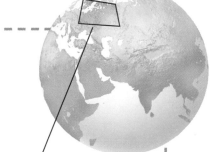

▲ *The gold crown of Kazan was part of the Imperial Crown jewels. It is covered with pearls and precious stones and has a band of sable fur.*

▲ *The Russian Imperial family were shot in the small town of Yekaterinburg near the Ural Mountains. Rumors persist today that Tsar Nicholas managed to hide some of his amazing fortune in a bank somewhere in Europe.*

LENIN AND THE RUSSIAN REVOLUTION

Following the assassination of the imperial family in July 1918, power in Russia passed to the leader of the Bolsheviks (Communist revolutionaries), Vladimir Lenin (1870-1924). Lenin had previously spent years in exile because of his opposition to the Tsar. His importance in Russian history is such that his embalmed body can still be viewed in a mausoleum in Red Square, Moscow.

▲ *An early revolutionary poster, 1917-1920, depicting the Bolshevik leader Vladimir Lenin addressing a crowd of supporters.*

RICHES FROM THE DEEP

▼ *All the sites in this section are named on the map below.*

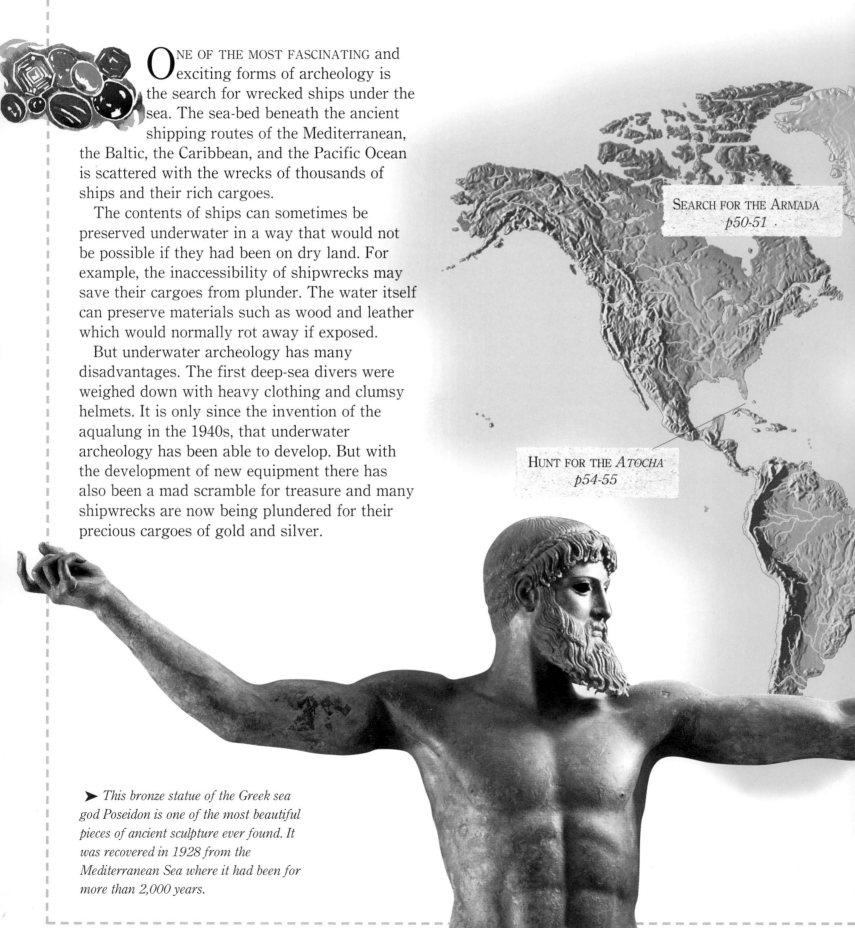

ONE OF THE MOST FASCINATING and exciting forms of archeology is the search for wrecked ships under the sea. The sea-bed beneath the ancient shipping routes of the Mediterranean, the Baltic, the Caribbean, and the Pacific Ocean is scattered with the wrecks of thousands of ships and their rich cargoes.

The contents of ships can sometimes be preserved underwater in a way that would not be possible if they had been on dry land. For example, the inaccessibility of shipwrecks may save their cargoes from plunder. The water itself can preserve materials such as wood and leather which would normally rot away if exposed.

But underwater archeology has many disadvantages. The first deep-sea divers were weighed down with heavy clothing and clumsy helmets. It is only since the invention of the aqualung in the 1940s, that underwater archeology has been able to develop. But with the development of new equipment there has also been a mad scramble for treasure and many shipwrecks are now being plundered for their precious cargoes of gold and silver.

SEARCH FOR THE ARMADA
p50-51 .

HUNT FOR THE *ATOCHA*
p54-55

➤ *This bronze statue of the Greek sea god Poseidon is one of the most beautiful pieces of ancient sculpture ever found. It was recovered in 1928 from the Mediterranean Sea where it had been for more than 2,000 years.*

◄ *Some of the 126 gold ingots from the* Geldermalsen *which sank in the China Sea in 1752. Along with 160,000 pieces of Chinese porcelain, the collection, called the Nanking Cargo, was sold in 1986.*

THE *MARY ROSE*
p52-53

THE *VASA*
p50-51

GRAVEYARD FOR SHIPS
p56-57

CARGOES FROM THE
EAST *p58-59*

WRECKS OF THE MEDITERRANEAN
p48-49

LOST TREASURE OF WORLD WAR II
p60-61

➤ *In 1960 the Swedish warship* Vasa *was raised from its watery grave at the bottom of Stockholm harbor where it had lain for more than three hundred and fifty years. The ship's wooden hull is now preserved in a special museum.*

SHIPWRECKS OF THE MEDITERRANEAN

FOR MORE THAN 3,000 YEARS the Mediterranean was one of the most important trading areas in the world. But many merchant ships sailing these waters never reached their destinations and the sea-bed is littered with their wrecked remains and the cargoes they were carrying.

The most common cargo carried across the Mediterranean in ancient times was large pottery storage jars called amphorae which were used for transporting wine, olive oil and other foods. The oldest ship found in the Mediterranean so far is a merchant ship dating to about 2500 B.C.

In A.D. 1900. some fishermen were diving for sponges off the small island of Antikythera lying between Crete and Greece. They found by chance some bronze and marble statues lying in the remains of a Roman cargo ship. An expedition was sent to recover the statues. Some of them dated to the fourth century B.C.

In the 1950s a sunken ship was found off the coast of Greece. A superb bronze figure of a boy jockey was brought up from the wreckage. Many years later, pieces of a bronze horse were recovered from the same place and after long painstaking work on reconstructing the horse, it was reunited with its jockey after 2,200 years.

◄ *A diver lifts an amphora out of the wreck of a Greek ship off the Turkish coast near Bodrum. This type of pottery vessel was the most common means of transporting wine and olive oil.*

EUROPE ASIA

FRANCE

ITALY GREECE Black Sea

SPAIN Mediterranean Athens Yassi Ada TURKEY
Sea

Mahdia ANTIKYTHERA CRETE CAPE
GELIDONYA

AFRICA Egypt

▲ *The ancient sea lanes of the Mediterranean criss-crossed their way from one shore to another. The places named on this map are the sites of ancient wrecks.*

◀ *Reconstruction of the seventh century ship found off the Turkish coast near Yassi Ada, as it might have looked when it sank in about A.D. 626. The ship was quite small, with a deck length of about 60 feet (18 meters) and could carry a cargo of about 50 tons. At the stern (back) can be seen a small square galley, while down below were stored the amphorae. The ship used a type of triangular sail named a lanteen and was steered with a rudder.*

The merchant ship of Yassi Ada

In the 1970s a Byzantine merchant ship was excavated off the Turkish coast at Yassi Ada. It had been carrying a cargo of amphorae filled with wine when it ran aground. Other objects found in the wreck included gold coins from the reign of the Emperor Heraclius who ruled A.D. 610-641.

◀ *This superb life-size bronze statue of the Greek sea god Poseidon was lifted out of the sea when fishing nets became caught up in its arms.*

SEARCH FOR THE ARMADA

I N MAY 1588 KING PHILIP II of Spain launched his great Armada against England. One hundred and thirty ships left Spain to conquer England but only sixty-three returned. When the ships reached the English Channel, they were attacked by a smaller, swifter English fleet. The huge, lumbering Spanish ships were chased all along the coast. The fleet was broken into smaller groups and single ships as they tried to limp back to Spain. Then a huge storm blew up which drove the remaining ships round the north of Scotland and Ireland. Many of them were smashed against rocks and sank.

Treasures of the *Girona*

Some of the wrecked ships of the Armada have been found and five of them have so far been excavated. One of the most interesting is the *Girona*. This ship had been carrying men rescued from other ships in the Armada and was dangerously overloaded. Far too heavy to reach Spain, the captain tried to find shelter off the west coast of Scotland. But the ship struck rocks on the coast of Ireland and sank. The wreck lay lost and forgotten for the next four hundred years.

In 1967 a Belgian diver called Robert Stenuit found the ship. Over three years his team brought up 12,000 objects, including huge cannons, bits of pottery, gold and silver coins, gold chains, beautiful lockets and pendants.

▲ *An English painting of the late sixteenth century. It shows the defeat of the Spanish Armada in 1588 by the fleet of smaller, faster English ships. The planned invasion of England by Spain never took place.*

▲ *Cameo in lapis lazuli with a portrait of a Roman emperor in profile, set within an ornate frame of gold and pearls. It was found in the wreck of the* Girona.

▶ *The coast of Northern Ireland. Some Spanish ships were blown round the British Isles and wrecked off Ireland and Scotland.*

▲ *The Armada was attacked in the English Channel. Some Spanish ships were driven by a storm round the north of Scotland and Ireland.*

PHILIP OF SPAIN AND HIS ARMADA

Philip II of Spain was a devout Roman Catholic. His second wife was his cousin, Queen Mary of England, but she died childless four years after their marriage. She was succeeded on the English throne by her Protestant half-sister Elizabeth I. Philip regarded Protestant England as a threat to his power so he planned to conquer England with his great Armada of 1588. But the Armada was scattered and wrecked off the coasts of Scotland and Ireland.

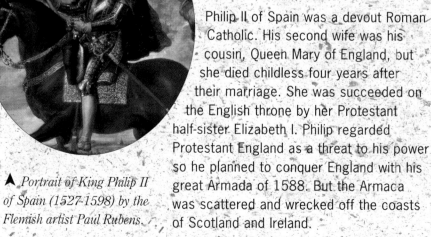

▲ *Portrait of King Philip II of Spain (1527-1598) by the Flemish artist Paul Rubens.*

▲ *One of the most beautiful of all the Girona treasures is this gold pendant. It is made in the form of a salamander and set with rubies. The salamander was once believed to be able to survive fires and this was probably worn as a charm to protect against fire. Many objects from the Girona can be seen in the Ulster Museum, Belfast.*

SINKING OF THE GREAT SHIPS

ON A CALM summer's day in July, 1545, a terrible sea tragedy took place before the horrified eyes of King Henry VIII of England. He had traveled from London to the harbor of Portsmouth on the south coast and was watching with his court as the English fleet sailed out to attack a huge French invasion force of 235 ships. Among the English vessels was the *Mary Rose*, the flagship of the navy and King Henry's pride. It was a large battleship and had just been refitted with powerful new guns designed to blow holes in enemy ships from a long range.

A disastrous refit

This refit proved disastrous as the *Mary Rose* was now very unbalanced, with heavy new guns and massive timbers needed to support the extra weight. In addition, the decks were crowded

▲ *A painting of the* Mary Rose, *painted a year after it sank on July 19, 1545. This is the only surviving contemporary picture of the ship and shows it after it has been refitted.*

with sailors, soldiers and archers. As the *Mary Rose* sailed out of Portsmouth, a sudden gust of wind blew and the ship began to tip violently over to one side. Water poured in through the gun ports and flooded the lower decks in seconds. The king and his courtiers watched helplessly as the *Mary Rose* sank in less than a minute. All but thirty of the seven hundred men on board perished.

The ship lay on the sea-bed for more than four centuries until modern technology was able to locate and raise it from the deep. In 1970, after years spent searching, a diving team led by Alexander McKee and Margaret Rule finally found the wreck. Inside the hull the divers found a rich treasure trove of 17,000 objects, from swords and bows and arrows to pewter plates, tankards, and pocket sundials.

RAISING THE *MARY ROSE*

In 1982, after 437 years on the sea-bed, the *Mary Rose* was raised to the surface. Wire ropes were fixed to the hull so the ship could be attached to a lifting frame. The frame lifted the ship off the bottom and it was moved into a steel cradle. The cradle containing the ship was then lifted on to a barge.

◄ *The* Mary Rose *is lifted on to a barge for transport ashore.*

▲ *The* Mary Rose *at the moment disaster struck. Water pours in through her lower open gunports and she is beginning to topple over and sink.*

◄ *Personal possessions found in the wreck of the* Mary Rose *include an embossed leather pouch, ivory comb, a seal, pocket sundial, gold coins and a rosary.*

➤ *Both the* Mary Rose *and the* Vasa *sank before the eyes of horrified on-lookers.*

•Southampton

Solent *Spithead* •Portsmouth

ISLE OF WIGHT **Mary Rose**

English Channel

SWEDEN Vasa
Stockholm •

THE RECOVERY OF THE VASA

The Swedish battleship *Vasa* sank in Stockholm harbor more than three hundred and fifty years ago. In 1959-1960 it was lifted off the sea-bed using barges filled with air and then floated into dock on its keel. The ship is now kept in a Stockholm museum.

▼ *The richly-decorated stern of the* Vasa, *seen in its specially-built museum.*

➤ *The Swedish warship* Vasa *after recovery, being brought into Stockholm harbor in 1960. This was the first time that a wooden warship had been raised almost intact more than three hundred and fifty years after it had sunk.*

HUNT FOR THE *ATOCHA*

Fore mast

Gunpowder and cannon ball stores

FOR MORE THAN TWO HUNDRED YEARS after Christopher Colombus sailed to the New World, huge Spanish galleons crossed the Atlantic Ocean carrying cargoes of gold and silver from South America to Spain. The sea off the coast of Florida was one of the most dangerous stages in the journey. On September 4, 1622 a convoy of twenty-eight ships left the Cuban port of Havana for Spain. A large galleon called the *Nuestra Senora de Atocha* was among them, its holds filled with treasures. But as it headed into the Straits of Florida, the convoy was hit by a hurricane and eight of the ships, including the *Atocha*, foundered and sank.

Finding the wreckage

The Spaniards soon located the *Atocha* because the ship still had its masts showing above the water. But divers were only able to recover two bronze cannons before another storm broke up the ship and scattered the remains across the bottom of the sea. For the next three hundred and fifty years the wreckage lay hidden. Modern efforts to find the *Atocha* began in the mid-1960s. The most determined attempt was made by American treasure-hunter, Mel Fisher. He searched for over ten years until, in 1973, he discovered thousands of silver coins and five coral-encrusted bronze cannons. Then, in 1985, the main wreckage was found. There were chests of silver coins and more than 500 silver ingots, each weighing 70 lbs (32kg). One chest was filled with solid gold bars and other treasures included heavy gold chains, and solid gold plates and cups.

▲ *One of the treasures from the* Atocha, *a gold and pearl cross.*

▲ *Huge treasure ships laden with gold and silver left parts of the New World for Spain. Some, such as the* Atocha, *never reached their destinations.*

Mizzen mast

Main mast

Captain's cabin

Rudder

Treasure rooms

Ship's stores

▼ *The wreckage of the Atocha was eventually found 20 miles (32meters) west of the original search area, near the Marquesas Keys, Florida.*

FLORIDA

Gulf of Mexico

Atocha

Atlantic

Marquesas Keys

Florida Keys

Straits of Florida

➤ Above right *a photograph taken under water showing one of the treasure chests from the Atocha with its precious contents.*

◄ *Mel Fisher with some of the treasure. He has spent much of his life searching for sunken treasure, but his greatest success was the recovery of the gold from Atocha.*

➤ *A solid gold plate with rich decoration found in the wreck.*

CARGOES FROM THE EAST

➤ Part of the Nanking Cargo, including blue and white dishes, cups and small bowls.

FROM 1600, for about two hundred years, merchant ships known as East Indiamen sailed across the oceans between Europe and China. From ports in the West they carried rich cargoes of gold and silver, lead, woolen cloth, and metal goods. They returned laden with spices from the East Indies, beautiful silks and porcelain from China, and tea, precious stones and cotton from India. They were the majestic trading vessels of the English East India Company and the Dutch East India Company.

Dangerous journeys

Their journeys were long and dangerous and many sank with their valuable cargoes. The English East India Company lost more than two hundred of its ships over two centuries and its Dutch rival also lost many. One of the Dutch East Indiamen to be lost was the *Hollandia* which sank off the Scilly Isles in 1743 on its way to the East. The ship was carrying 130,000 guilders (about U.S. $77,860) worth of silver coins and everything, including the entire crew, went down. The cargo was recovered in the 1970s. In 1752, another Dutch East Indiaman named the *Geldermalsen* was traveling from China back to Holland. On board was a huge collection of Chinese porcelain, gold ingots, tea and raw silk. As it sailed across the South China Sea, it hit a submerged reef of rocks and slowly began to sink. By dawn of the next morning the ship had disappeared beneath the waves and only a few of the crew managed to survive.

In 1985, the wreck of the *Geldermalsen* was found and the recovery of its contents began. But what was brought to the surface after more than 230 years on the sea-bed was beyond anyone's expectations. Among the wreckage, the divers found 126 ingots of Chinese gold. Even more spectacular was an almost complete haul of Chinese export porcelain. It had been shipped from the port of Nanking and has come to be known as the "Nanking Cargo." It was also remarkable because so much of it had survived unbroken. In the end about 160,000 pieces of porcelain were recovered.

THE EAST INDIA COMPANIES

The English and Dutch East India Companies were founded to break the control the Portuguese had over trade with the East. The English company was founded in 1600 and the Dutch company two years later. Throughout the 17th and 18th centuries there was a lot of rivalry between the two companies which sometimes led to fierce trade wars.

➤ A view of Hong Kong harbor in about 1820. The port grew rich from trade between East and West and still plays a vital part in world trade.

58

▼ European trade with the Far East formed the most important business of the East India Companies.

PORCELAIN FOR EXPORT

During the 17th and 18th centuries, Chinese blue-and-white porcelain became very popular in Europe. It was made for export at Ching-te-chen and then shipped to Europe in vast quantities from the port of Nanking. Western dealers gave it the name "Nanking porcelain" during the 19th century.

◄ A teapot from the Geldermalsen. *Tea in the 18th century was extremely expensive and only the rich could afford to drink it.*

▼ *Intense trade rivalry led to sea battles between the Dutch and English. This picture shows the Battle of La Hogue in 1692.*

LOST TREASURE OF WORLD WAR II

IN LATE NOVEMBER 1941, Japan began assembling a huge force of warships, aircraft carriers and airplanes near an island called Kunashiri. From there the force began to sail towards Hawaii. Then on December 7, 1941, the Japanese burst into World War II with a surprise attack on the U.S. Pacific Fleet based at Pearl Harbor on the Hawaiian island of Oahu.

Wave upon wave of Japanese airplanes bombed the port. The ships in the harbor and the airplanes in the airfields were easy targets. More than 3,000 U.S. servicemen were killed or wounded and the U.S. fleet was put out of action.

False mercy mission

By the beginning of 1945, the Japanese were losing all the territories they had conquered since their attack on Pearl Harbor. An extraordinary incident happened at this time.

The Japanese were given permission to transport wounded soldiers back to Japan. One ship running these mercy missions named the *Awa Maru,* set out from Southeast Asia with 2,000 wounded on board. But the ship was also carrying an incredible fortune in stolen treasure. The Japanese had plans to smuggle this loot to Japan where it would be used to revive their war effort. The treasure is believed to have included art treasures, diamonds, 12 tons of precious platinum metal, 40 tons of gold, 2,000 tons of tungsten and 3,000 tonnes of tin.

The *Awa Maru* had nearly reached Japan when it met a U.S. submarine lurking in the Straits of Formosa. The submarine fired and the *Awa Maru* sank with the loss of all the wounded soldiers on board and the treasure. It has lain at the bottom of the sea, 14 miles (22.5 kilometers) off the Chinese coast ever since, and all attempts to recover it have been unsuccessful.

◄ *Admiral Isoroku Yamamoto was commander-in chief of the Japanese navy. He was one of the planners of the attack on Pearl Harbor. He was killed in 1943.*

▼ *The Japanese battleship* Yamato *on trial in the Sea of Japan in 1941. Shortly after this photograph was taken the Japanese attacked the U.S. naval base of Pearl Harbor.*

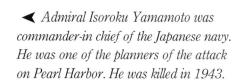

▼ *The cargo ship* Awa Maru *was torpedoed by a U.S. submarine in 1954 and sank off the Straits of Formosa.*

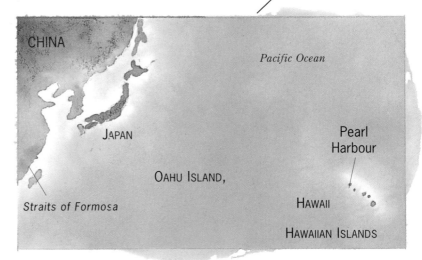

CHINA

Pacific Ocean

JAPAN

OAHU ISLAND,

Straits of Formosa

Pearl Harbour

HAWAII

HAWAIIAN ISLANDS

▲ *U.S. military police guard over U.S. $6 million of silver and platinum bars. At the end of the war Japan's own gold reserves were captured and confiscated.*

▼ *Pearl Harbor under attack on December 7, 1941. Many ships were sunk including the giant U.S.S. Arizona and a number of smaller ships were destroyed or badly damaged.*

THE ATTACK ON PEARL HARBOR

The scale of the disaster at Pearl Harbor and the way the United States military was caught by surprise created an uproar. The navy and army commanders were sacked and an investigation began. It found that while the United States officials had been aware that Japan would probably attack, they did not know when or where it would take place.

STOLEN TREASURE

 **W**AR AND PLUNDER have always marched together side-by-side. When a country was conquered or a city captured in war, the victorious armies would go on the rampage, looting and killing. The losers in the war were considered fair game and the soldiers were free to grab what they could. It was their reward for being on the winning side.

Symbols of triumph and victory

There is another, more official kind of looting which has an equally ancient history. The leaders of victorious armies would take the treasures of the conquered state which then formed important symbols of their victory. Roman generals took personal trophies to decorate their triumphal processions back in Rome. When Queen Zenobia of Palmyra was defeated by the Romans in A.D. 272, she was the star attraction in the Emperor Aurelian's triumphal procession. Along with the wagons of looted treasure she was led through the streets of Rome, "in sumptuous bondage," weighed down with chains of solid gold. There was yet another type of loot – great works of art stolen for the greater glory of the victorious nation. It was as if by obtaining these treasures the victors thought they would inherit the ancient and noble characteristics of the conquered people.

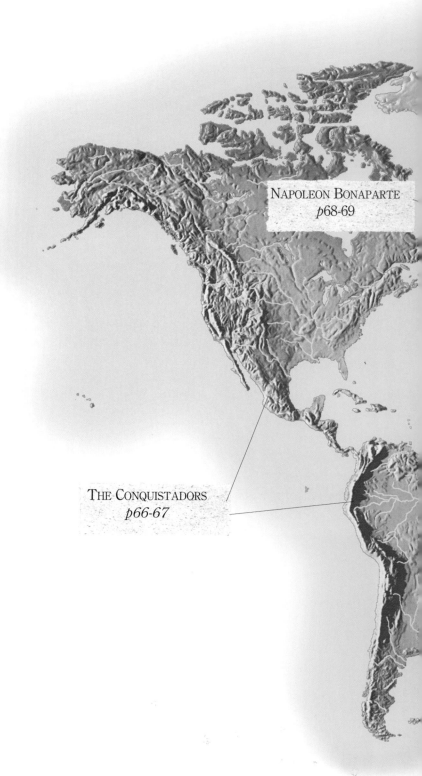

NAPOLEON BONAPARTE
p68-69

THE CONQUISTADORS
p66-67

◀ *These bronze horses from the front of St Mark's Cathedral in Venice, Italy, were originally stolen by the Venetians from Constantinople in 1204. They were stolen again by Napoleon and taken to France before they were finally returned to Venice when he fell from power.*

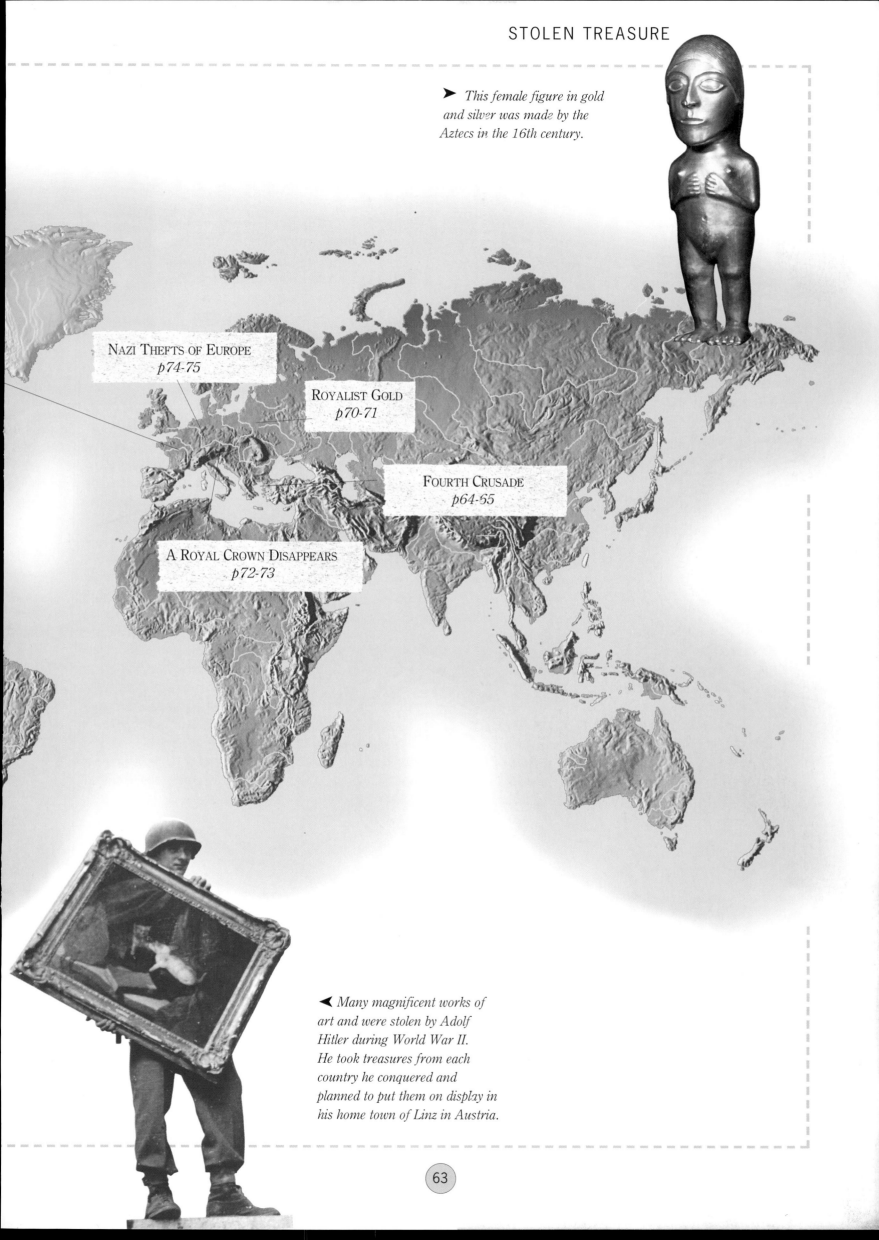

➤ *This female figure in gold and silver was made by the Aztecs in the 16th century.*

NAZI THEFTS OF EUROPE
p74-75

ROYALIST GOLD
p70-71

FOURTH CRUSADE
p64-65

A ROYAL CROWN DISAPPEARS
p72-73

◄ *Many magnificent works of art and were stolen by Adolf Hitler during World War II. He took treasures from each country he conquered and planned to put them on display in his home town of Linz in Austria.*

FOURTH CRUSADE

OWARDS THE END of the 11th century, a fierce Muslim people from Turkey called the Seljuks attacked the borders of the Byzantine empire, successor to the ancient Roman empire in the East. When they captured the holy city of Jerusalem, the Byzantine emperor Alexius I asked for help from the Pope. As head of the Roman Catholic Church, Pope Urban II called for a Christian army to come to the aid of the Emperor Alexius and recapture Jerusalem. This call to arms in 1095 marks the beginning of the Crusades, a series of holy wars fought by Christians against Muslims. They lasted for nearly two hundred years from 1095 until 1291

The Fourth Crusade begins

One of the strangest chapters in the history of the Crusades was that of the Fourth Crusade. In 1198, Pope Innocent III called for a Christian army to invade Egypt. The rich merchant city of Venice was asked to provide ships for transport. The Venetians were not interested in attacking Egypt because they had strong trading links with that country. They were more interested in attacking Constantinople (now Istanbul), the capital city of the Byzantine empire and Venice's main trading rival. As the Crusaders could not afford to pay for the Venetian ships, they agreed that instead of attacking Egypt they would help the Venetians to capture the Hungarian city of Zara and then move against Constantinople.

In the summer of 1203 Constantinople was surrounded and fell, Emperor Alexius III was deposed and a new emperor placed on the throne. But the people of Constantinople assassinated the new emperor which infuriated the Crusaders and the Venetians, who proceeded to take their revenge. For three terrible days, from April 13, 1204, Constantinople was subjected to massacres and looting by a barbaric mob of soldiers. Many priceless works of art, icons and religious relics, and other treasures of gold, silver and precious stones were destroyed. But many more were stolen and taken back to western Europe, a large number of them were taken to Venice.

▲ *Constantinople's imperial family watch a chariot race at the hippodrome (open-air stadium). The bronze horses which once crowned the imperial box were stolen by Crusaders and taken to Venice, Italy.*

THE CITY OF CANALS

Venice was once a powerful merchant city with trading links all round the Mediterranean. It was built on 118 islands with 180 canals running between them. It is a very beautiful city and famous buildings include St Mark's Cathedral, the Doge's Palace and the Bridge of Sighs.

▶ *The taking of Constantinople by the Crusaders in 1204. A painting made in 1840 by the French artist Eugene Delacroix.*

◀ *St Mark's Basilica in Venice. Many of the treasures stolen from Constantinople were brought back to Venice and can be seen in this church.*

◄ *The seige of Constantinople by the Turks. The sacking of the city by the Crusaders severely weakened it and led to its capture by the Turks in 1453.*

▲ *The Crusades were a series of holy wars fought by Christians from Europe to capture Jerusalem and the Holy Land from the Muslims. They lasted from 1095-1291.*

THE CONQUISTADORS

IN 1519 THE SPANISH governor of Cuba appointed a soldier and adventurer named Hernan Cortes to lead an expedition to explore the American mainland. Cortes gathered a band of about five hundred men, most of them unemployed soldiers looking for a fortune. This small army set sail from Havana and landed on the coast of Mexico, which at that time was part of the huge Aztec empire.

A golden helmet

As the Spaniards marched inland, Cortes sent a messenger on ahead with gifts for the Aztec emperor, Montezuma. One of the presents was a Spanish helmet. The emperor sent presents in return. He was very anxious that the Spaniards should go no further and hoped his gifts would buy them off. One of his presents was the same helmet filled to its top with grains of gold. But if Montezuma thought this would persuade the Spaniards not to come any further he was very wrong. It had the opposite effect and whetted their insatiable appetite for gold.

▲ *A gold and silver female figure made by the Aztecs in the 15th century.*

A treasury of gold

When they reached the Aztec capital city of Tenochtitlan the Spaniards were received by Montezuma and housed in one of his palaces.

Unfortunately for the Aztecs this building also contained the emperor's treasury and when the Spaniards discovered this they broke in. They found rooms piled to the ceiling with gold, silver and precious stones. A Spanish priest wrote, "When they saw the quantity of golden objects – jewels and plates and ingots — which lay in those chambers they were quite transported." The Spaniards took the emperor prisoner, and began raiding his treasury.

When Cortes was away from the city one day the soldiers he had left behind tried to stop an important Aztec religious ceremony. Cortes returned to find the city in uproar and his soldiers under siege in the palace. He sent Montezuma to calm the Aztecs but they turned on their emperor and stoned him to death. The Spaniards tried to escape from Tenochtitlan at night, but as they were crossing a canal they were attacked by Aztec soldiers and many of them were drowned, weighed down by the huge amounts of gold that they were carrying.

Cortes escaped and regrouped with more soldiers and advanced on Tenochtitlan. The Aztecs were defeated and the Spaniards destroyed the city killing all the inhabitants. All the treasure the Spaniards found was sent back to Spain.

DEATH OF AN INCA EMPEROR

When the Inca emperor, Atahualpa, first met the Spaniards they took him prisoner and his followers were slaughtered. He offered to buy his freedom by filing a room 17 x 22 feet (5 x 7 meters) with gold and other treasures. But once this incredible ransom was paid, Atahualpa was murdered by the Spanish.

◄ *The city of Ollantaytambo, near Cuzco in Peru. This was one of the last cities to be built by the Incas before they were conquered in 1532 by the Spaniards led by Francisco Pizarro.*

▼ After the Spaniards had conquered the Aztec empire in Mexico and the Inca empire in Peru, expeditions were sent out to all parts of the Americas in the hope of finding more gold and treasure.

▲ An illustration from a German book of 1602 showing a Spaniard on a llama and carrying stolen treasure. He is with two local guides.

◄ This double-headed serpent was probably worn in an Aztec religious ceremony as part of a headdress. It is made of wood and covered in small pieces of turquoise.

▼ Montezuma, emperor of the Aztecs. He was held hostage by the Spaniards before being killed by his own people.

▼ The last battle between the Aztecs and the Spanish conquistadors. With the destruction of their capital city of Tenochtitlan, the Aztec empire collapsed.

NAPOLEON, EMPEROR OF FRANCE

Out of the blood and chaos of the French Revolution came one of the most brilliant soldiers the world has ever seen and who led one of the biggest looting operations in history. Napoleon Bonaparte became leader of the new French Republic in 1799 and his rise to power was completed in 1804 when he was crowned Emperor of the French. In 1796, as commander of the French army, Napoleon successfully attacked Italy. During the next eighteen months he carried out an incredible campaign of stealing treasures. His explanation was that, "the French Republic is the only country in the world which can give a safe home to these master-pieces." While non-Frenchmen regarded this as common theft, Napoleon and his helpers declared that

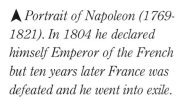

▲ *Portrait of Napoleon (1769-1821). In 1804 he declared himself Emperor of the French but ten years later France was defeated and he went into exile.*

they were simply collecting what was theirs by conquest. Treaties signed with local Italian rulers forced them to hand over particular works of art. Milan was looted and then finally Rome. Pope Pius VI was forced to hand over antique sculptures and a hundred paintings. Despite Italian fury at this robbery the pieces were shipped off to France. Next was the city of Venice, and there Napoleon and his art advisers chose more paintings and sculptures. They took the bronze horses of St Mark, stolen by the Venetians when they sacked Constantinople in 1204 (see page 64). As French conquests in Europe continued, so the list of stolen treasures grew. Paintings, gold, silver, books, holy relics and sculptures were packed off to Paris where they remained for twenty years until Napoloen's defeat in 1815. Most of the treasures were gradually returned, but the hoard was so enormous that ownership of some pieces was disputed and some of them are still in France to this day.

FRANCE AND THE EGYPTIAN STYLE

In 1798 Napoleon led an expedition to Egypt. He took with him 175 scholars including an art historian called Baron Denon. Denon was very impressed by the art and architecture of Egypt and on his return to France published a book on the subject. This had a great influence on the artistic styles of Europe during the next century.

◄ *The famous bronze horses from St Mark's Cathedral, Venice, Italy. Napoleon stole these and many other treasures, and took them back to France.*

► *A cartoon of about 1800 showing Napoleon fleeing from Egypt after being defeated at the battle of the Nile.*

The map shows:

Moscow •
RUSSIA

London •

• Paris   Napoleon's empire at its height

FRANCE   • Vienna

          Milan •   • Venice   Black Sea

SPAIN   CORSICA   • Rome

          ITALY

Parma   SYRIA

          Mediterrean Sea

               • Syene

          EGYPT

▲ By 1810 the French empire spread across most of Europe, and treasures and works of art were being shipped from the conquered lands back to France.

◄ The French army halts at Syene in Egypt. By this time Napoleon was in Syria trying to create an empire in the East.

➤ The famous sculpture of Laocöon, a priest of Troy, with his two sons. This ancient work of art was carried off from Rome to Paris in 1796, but returned in 1814 after the defeat of Napoleon.

ROYALIST GOLD

T SAR NICHOLAS II was the last emperor of Russia. He was forced to abdicate at the end of 1917, and six months later he and his family were murdered in a house in Siberia. The new rulers of Russia were the Communist Bolsheviks who had led the revolution which overthrew the Tsar. But for a number of years following the revolution, fighting continued between the Communist Red Army and the White Army of royalists who remained loyal to the cause of the dead emperor. The Communist government of Russia was regarded as a major threat by many European countries and they sent troops and money to support the White Russians. The commander of the White Army in the north was Admiral Alexander Kolchak, who was based in Siberia. General Anton Denikin commanded the White Army in the south, from an area round the Black Sea. The White Russians needed a lot

▲ *The storming of the Winter Palace in Petrograd (St Petersburg) in October 1917. Shortly after this the last Tsar of Russia, Nicholas II, was forced to abdicate.*

of money to maintain their fight against the Communists. Admiral Kolchak was thought to have amassed an amazing five hundred tons of gold taken from the imperial treasury in the Kremlin, Moscow. Many aristocratic supporters of the White Russians had donated their own fortunes to help the cause. General Denikin had a smaller fund which included 450 lbs (200 kgs) of platinum and bags of gold coins and precious stones. Financed by this fortune, the White Army came close to defeating their enemies. But finally the Reds gained the upper hand and Kolchak and his forces were surrounded. He was captured and executed. At this point his incredible treasure disappeared. It may be that Kolchak hid it before he was captured. One story claims that it lies at the bottom of Lake Baikal, the deepest lake in the world. General Denikin continued to fight on for another year, but by 1920 he and his troops were also on the run, pursued by the Communists. His smaller hoard of treasure was much easier to transport and he probably took it with him out of Russia. But what happened to it after that remains a mystery.

▶ *The Red Army enters Odessa in 1919. The Russian Civil War was at its height and it was to be at least another year before the Red Army and the Bolsheviks gained control. But for some months the opposing White Army seemed close to victory.*

WHITE RUSSIANS IN EXILE

After the defeat of the White Army by the Communists, many White Russians who supported the imperial family left Russia and went permanently into exile. Many of them settled in Britain or France and never returned to their homeland.

◀ *Admiral Kolchak (1874-1920) appointed himself supreme ruler of Russia in October 1918. He was eventually captured and shot.*

◄ *The Russian civil war1917-1920 was fought across Russia and Central Asia*

▲ *Units of the First Mounted Army crossing the Dneiper river near Kakhovka in October 1920. By this time the White Army was on the run and close to total defeat.*

➤ *The first cavalry regiment of the Red Army marches through Petrograd in 1918. The city was renamed Leningrad after the leader of the Bolsheviks, Vladimir Lenin. But in 1991 the old name of St Petersburg was restored once more.*

A ROYAL CROWN DISAPPEARS

IN NOVEMBER 1944, World War II was ending and the Soviet Red Army was marching towards Budapest, the capital of Hungary. For much of the war Hungary had been under the control of Nazi Germany and now it was the turn of the Nazis to flee. On a platform of the Budapest railway station was the Nazi prime minister of Hungary, Ferenc Szalasi, and with him were crates full of gold and jewels.

A large black chest had been brought on to the train by an armed guard. Inside was the Crown of St Stephen. According to legend, this had been given to St Stephen, the first king of Hungary, by Pope Sylvester II in about A.D. 1000. This gave the crown a special significance in the eyes of the Hungarians, it was regarded as the true symbol of power in Hungary.

Crown jewels found and lost

The crown had had a very chequered history. It had been hidden, captured or stolen a number of times. In May 1945, a group of Hungarians traveling with a large locked chest was detained by U.S. soldiers in Bavaria. When the chest was opened it was found to be empty. But after interrogation, the Hungarians admitted that the crown and other regalia had been hidden in a barrel in a marsh near the village of Mattsee. The marsh was searched and the crown jewels fished out and sent to a bank in Frankfurt where they were locked up once more. And that, for the next twenty years, was the end of the story, for the Crown of St Stephen completely vanished.

◀ *A postage stamp issued in Hungary to celebrate the return of the Crown of St Stephen to Budapest in January, 1978. The crown with its bent cross, is seen with the rest of the royal regalia stolen more than thirty-three years earlier.*

▲ *The Crown of St Stephen is the symbol of Hungary. It has had an adventurous history – it has been stolen, lost and hidden away before being finally returned to its homeland by the United States government in 1978.*

▲ *In this painting St Stephen receives the Crown of Hungary from Pope. Sylvester II. It was supposed to have been given to him at his coronation in A.D. 1000.*

▼ *A view of the Citadel of Budapest from the Chain Bridge. The bridge is one of many that cross the river Danube and link the two cities of Buda and Pesth together to form the capital of Hungary.*

RETURN OF THE CROWN

In August 1965, after years of rumor, the United States government officially admitted that the crown was in its safe-keeping in Fort Knox. But it refused to return this national symbol while Hungary was still ruled by Communist dictators. Finally, almost exactly thirty years after it had left Budapest on the train, on November 4, 1977, the Crown of St Stephen and other royal regalia were formally handed back to the Hungarians by the American Secretary of State in January 1978.

NAZI THEFTS OF EUROPE

ADOLF HITLER stole for his country. He believed that the victorious German armies of World War II had a right to plunder the museums, banks and private art collections of Europe. This official robbery was even given its own code name: Special Operation Linz. It was so-called because Hitler planned to make his home town of Linz in Austria the cultural center of the world. This small town was going to be completely rebuilt with a museum and art gallery stuffed with looted treasures.

Storehouses packed with treasure

Even as Hitler's empire started collapsing, the plunder of Europe continued right up to the last days of the war. Paintings, gold and silverware, sculptures, jewelry, books, furniture, carpets, and tapestries were cataloged, photographed, and packed into boxes and stored in secret locations. The advancing Soviet, British and U.S. armies discovered these storehouses of treasures. Over two years British treasure-hunters unearthed 1,800 tons of stolen objects, from paintings to prehistoric artefacts. One of the most incredible discoveries was made in a salt mine at Alt Aussee in the Austrian Tyrol. Inside the huge underground chambers, shelves stretched in all directions. Stacked on these shelves was an amazing collection of ancient sculptures, superb paintings, church furnishings and jewelry. All these treasures were waiting to be housed in Hitler's museum at Linz.

▲ *A cupboard at the Castle of Velderstein full of stolen treasures – gold and silver bowls, and candlesticks from churches and private homes.*

▲ *Neunschwanstein Castle perched on a mountainside at Fussen on the German border with Switzerland. A fortune in stolen works of art was found inside.*

◄ Hundreds of
valuable paintings
were found in
Neunschwanstein.
This painting being
carried away is by
an 18th century
French artist named
Jean-Baptist Chardin.

Baltic Sea

Berlin •

GERMANY

Neunschwanstein
Castle

Danube

Lenz

Alps   Austrian Tyrol   Vienna

AUSTRIA

◄ Adolf Hitler took
precious works of art,
sculptures, gold and
silver, and other treasures
from every country in
Europe that he conquered.
They were stored away in
hidden locationswaiting
to be displayed in Hitler's
museum in Linz
in Austria.

➤ Excavations being carried out in the
grounds of the castle to uncover even
more treasures hidden underground.

HAVE ALL THE STOLEN TREASURES BEEN RETURNED?

With the end of the war came the difficult task of returning the treasures
to their rightful owners. About four-fifths were found and given back to the
museums and private collectors the rest
remains hidden somewhere.

◄ ➤ Left some of the silver stolen from Jewish
synagogues. Right Hermann Goering added
precious 16th century Italian jewelry to his collection of
stolen treasures. In 1942 he told German troops, "Whenever
you come across anything that may be needed by the German
people you must be after it like bloodhounds. It must be
brought to Germany."

ROMANTIC RUMORS

For as long as there are hidden treasures still to be found there will be people ready to risk their lives and fortunes to go in search of them. Occupying a place between fact and fiction are those stories about fantastic buried treasures awaiting discovery. For centuries people have wanted to believe that the stories are true and that the treasures really do exist. These are the treasures of myth and legend surrounded by suggestion and rumor. Their fame rests upon a word or a vague story mentioned in passing. The stories are passed down from one generation to the next and usually with each telling the facts become more hazy and the legendary treasure becomes ever more fabulous

Legends of buried treasure

Legends about incredible buried treasures abound from East to West, from Japan to the Americas. One of the most famous concerns El Dorado, "the golden one," of Latin America. These heavily embroidered tales have fired the imaginations of countless people down the centuries and many of them have lost fortunes of their own in their relentless pursuit of dazzling riches. Some have become so obsessed by fantastic stories of buried treasure that they have even committed murder to prevent others from reaching it first.

The facts, however, usually show that most of these stories have little basis in truth. But the more distant and fantastic the stories are, the more people are bewitched by them and are prepared to risk everything in their quest. The search for these legendary treasures of myth and romance continues today.

➤ *One of the most enduring stories of hidden treasure is that of El Dorado, "the golden one." This is a gold model of a raft believed to have been used in the El Dorado ceremony.*

BLACKBEARD AND THE DEVIL'S SECRET
p86-87

LITTLE BIG HORN
p90-91

CURSE OF THE THUNDER GOD
p88-89

QUEST FOR EL DORADO
p80-81

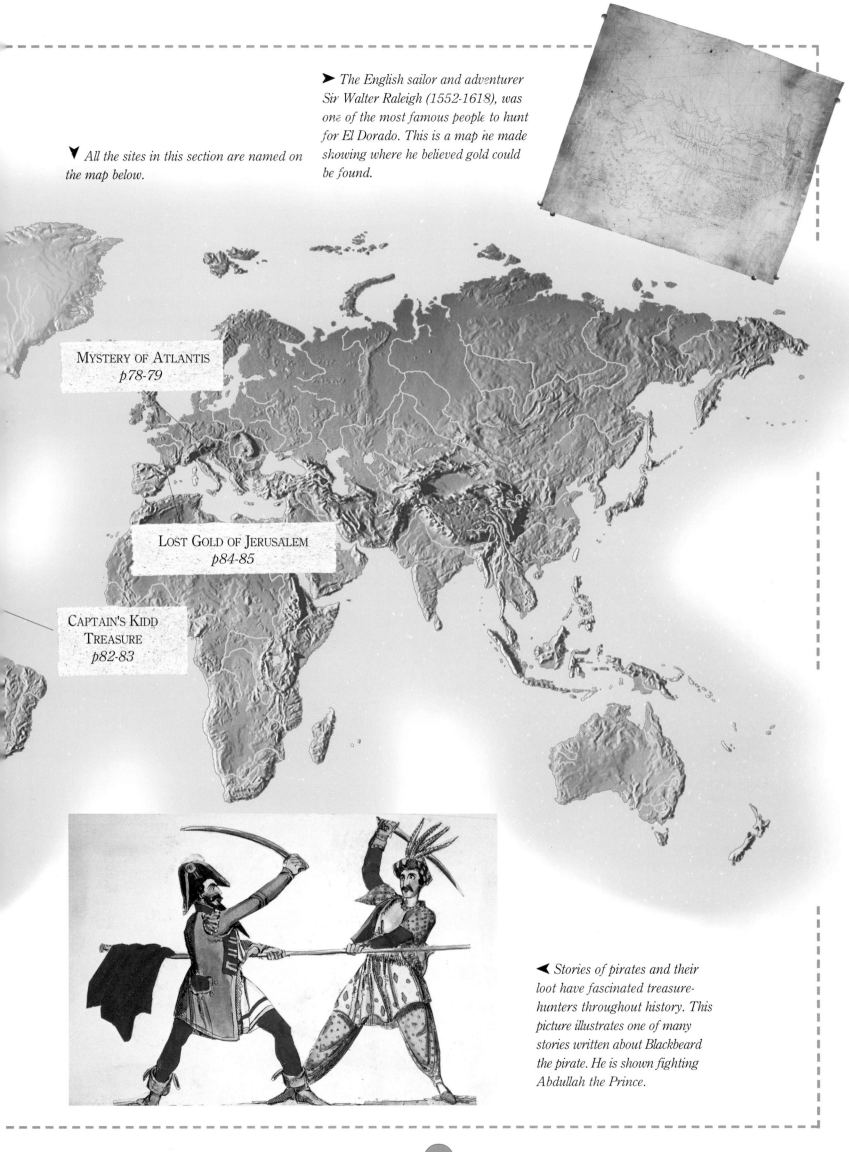

➤ The English sailor and adventurer Sir Walter Raleigh (1552-1618), was one of the most famous people to hunt for El Dorado. This is a map he made showing where he believed gold could be found.

▼ All the sites in this section are named on the map below.

MYSTERY OF ATLANTIS
p78-79

LOST GOLD OF JERUSALEM
p84-85

CAPTAIN'S KIDD
TREASURE
p82-83

◄ Stories of pirates and their loot have fascinated treasure-hunters throughout history. This picture illustrates one of many stories written about Blackbeard the pirate. He is shown fighting Abdullah the Prince.

MYSTERY OF ATLANTIS

THE LOST LAND OF ATLANTIS was first recorded by the Greek philospher Plato in about 355 B.C. in two books: *Timaeus* and *Critias*. According to Plato, Atlantis was a very large island rich in minerals and precious metals such as gold. The capital city was circular – about 14 miles (22 kilometers) in diameter. In the center of the city was a hill where the royal palace and main temple stood. In about 355 b.c. Plato wrote the palace was, "covered all over with gold and silver," while in the temple were huge gold statues of the sea god Poseidon, "standing in a chariot drawn by six winged horses."

Plato writes how happy the people of Atlantis were, and how fair and tolerant their society. But they became greedy for more gold. Zeus, the chief god of the Greeks, decided to punish them. "In a single dreadful day and night," the great civilization of Atlantis and all its riches were swept beneath the sea by Zeus's fury because of the wickedness of its people.

Some archeologists today suggest Plato's story may in fact contain some truth. In the 15th century B.C., the island of Thera (Santorini), 74 miles (120 kilometers) to the north of Crete, was destroyed in a huge volcanic explosion. Its destruction caused devastation on nearby Crete and the archeologists point to evidence that the Minoan civilization of Crete collapsed at about the same time. They suggest the destruction of the palace of Knossos on Crete was caused by volcanic ash and debris. So Plato's story of Atlantis may be an account of the disappearance of the Cretan civilization 800 years earlier.

▲ *Excavations at the site of Akrotiri on the island of Thera (Santorini), thought by some to be the lost city of Atlantis. The town was built by the Minoans from the nearby island of Crete.*

THE DESTRUCTION OF THERA

1 The Greek island of Thera before the volcanic eruption blew it apart in about 1470 B.C.

2 Thera after the eruption of the volcano on the western side of the island.

3 Some time after the explosion the whole western part of the island sank into the sea, leaving it a crescent shape.

➤ The precise location of the city of Atlantis remains a mystery. In the 16th century one writer suggested that America should be renamed Atlantis. Other people claim the city formed a bridge of land between Europe and America and acted as an avenue for ancient American civilizations.

UNITED STATES OF AMERICA

Atlantic Ocean

Santorini (Thera)

Gibraltar

AFRICA

Bimini

The Azores

SOUTH AMERICA

➤ An artist's impression of the lost city of Atlantis based on the description by Plato. The circular city was surrounded by canals and horse races were held around the walls.

▲ A view of the cliffs of Santorini today. The island has become a popular holiday destination and many cruise ships stop there.

The Myth of the Minotaur

The Minotaur was a monster with the body of a man and the head of a bull. It was kept in the center of a labyrinth, or maze, on the island of Crete. Every nine years it was given seven youths and seven maidens from Athens to eat. The Minotaur was finally killed by the hero Theseus with the help of Ariadne, daughter of King Minos of Crete.

QUEST FOR EL DORADO

IN 1519 HERNAN CORTES conquered the fabulously rich Aztec empire, and in 1532 Francisco Pizarro took the even richer empire of the Incas. This resulted in an incredible stream of gold, silver and precious stones into Spain from Mexico and Peru. The Spanish conquistadors found people using gold tools and heard tales of the golden riches of a mysterious king. This was El Dorado, "the golden one" who ruled a mountain kingdom where gold was as common as dust.

What really caught the imaginations of the Spaniards were accounts from local people of a royal ceremony. Each year the king was covered, "with a sticky earth on which they placed gold dust so that he was completely covered with this metal." He was placed on a raft surrounded by gold and emeralds and the raft was rowed out into a sacred lake. When it reached the center, the gold-covered king made his offerings to the gods, "throwing out all the piles gold and emeralds into the middle of the lake."

The legend of El Dorado was based on fact. A wealthy and powerful kingdom had existed in the eastern part of the Andes Mountains and the people had worshiped their gods at Lake Guatavita, in modern Colombia. But by the time the Spaniards arrived in the Americas the kingdom had disappeared.

◀ A gold tumi or ceremonial knife with a semi-circular blade decorated with turquoise. It was made by craftsmen of the Chimu people of northern Peru. Their metalsmiths were so highly regarded that they went to work for the Inca emperor when the Chimu were conquered by the Incas in 1470.

▼ An engraving of 1654 showing the Muisca people of Colombia coating their chieftan in gold dust. This European picture was based on the stories the conquistadors heard about the El Dorado ceremony.

THE LEGEND CONTINUES

The legend of El Dorado grew until it was estimated that fifty million golden objects lay beneath Lake Guatavita. Another version of the legend claimed that the king lived in a city made of gold. The first group of conquistadors reached Lake Guatavita in 1539 but they found no golden city and moved on. The Spanish were so sure that El Dorado existed they named the land between the Andes and the Orinoco river the Province of El Dorado.

▲ *El Dorado may have been located in the eastern part of the Andes Mountains The legend grew until it was estimated that fifty million golden objects lay beneath Lake Guatavita.*

▲ *Lake Guatavita in Colombia, lying at 9,843 feet (3,000 meters) in the Andes Mountains. A Spanish merchant attempted to recover gold from the lake by taking a deep slice out of the rim on the far side to drain away the water. He managed to find some objects but the side of the trench collapsed killing hundreds of workmen. The merchant himself was bankrupted in his search for gold, and in 1962, the Colombian government stopped any more expeditions and declared Lake Guatavita a protected area.*

▶ *This gold model of a raft with figures on it is believed to show part of the actual El Dorado ceremony. The "golden one" stands tall at the back, surrounded by his attendants who will help him throw offerings of gold and emeralds into the sacred lake. The model was one of the valuable objects recovered from Lake Guatavita.*

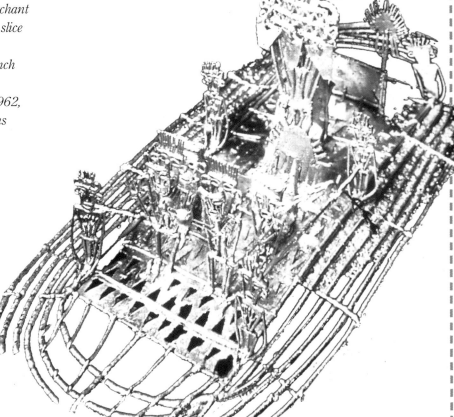

CAPTAIN KIDD'S TREASURE

WILLIAM KIDD was born in Scotland in about 1650. He joined the British navy as a boy and was soon fighting against the French in the West Indies.

Kidd becomes a pirate

In 1695, Kidd was commanded by the English king William III, to arrest pirates and to confiscate their booty. After several months of failure, Kidd sailed to Madagascar and decided to join the very pirates he was supposed to be hunting down. In his new role, he attacked several ships in the Indian Ocean. One of these was the *Quedagh Merchant* which was carrying a cargo worth about $109,000.

Kidd was now a wanted man and had earned a reputation for being bold and ruthless. But instead of going on the run he decided to try and clear his name. He turned himself over to Lord Bellamont, the governor of Long Island and one of his patrons, whereupon he was immediately arrested and sent back to London to stand trial. Meanwhile, Lord Bellamont stole $21,800 worth of Kidd's booty while Kidd's own crew stole the rest and set fire to his ship.

Kidd's treasure remains hidden

In a desperate attempt to escape execution, Kidd offered to lead his captors to where, he claimed, his treasure was hidden. He even tried to bribe his executioner with the promise of riches. But these attempts to save his life failed and he was hanged in London on May 23, 1701. His body was left hanging from the gallows for many days afterwards.

With each telling of the tale of Captain Kidd's treasure its value was exaggerated further. Over the years it has been hunted in the most unlikely places, from New York to the islands of Japan, some of the areas thousands of miles from anywhere that Kidd actually visited. Kidd's treasure almost certainly does not exist, but still there are people who are prepared to spend fortunes in their pursuit of his mythical loot.

◄ ➤ Left *Captain Kidd before the bar of the House of Commons, London, March 1701. From here he was sent for trial and was found guilty of piracy and murder.* Right *The body of Captain Kidd was left hanging from a gibbet, "as a great terror to all persons from committing the like crimes."*

UNITED STATES
OF AMERICA

Long Island

Florida

Atlantic Ocean

CUBA

Caribbean Sea

WEST
INDIES

The ORDINARY of NEWGATE his Account of the Behaviour, Confessions, and Dying-Words of Captain William Kidd, and other Pirates, that were Executed at the Execution-Dock in Wapping, on Friday May 23, 1701.

▲ *One of the most important additions to the legend of Captain Kidd's treasure was this letter written shortly before his death. In it he wrote, "I have lodged goods and treasures to the value of $125,000 (£100,000) in the Indies."*

The Hunt Continues

For more than two hundred years people have searched for Captain Kidd's treasure. A hoard of gold and silver was found on a remote Japanese island in 1956. The legend of Kidd's treasure was so famous that people said this must be it, even although Kidd had never been anywhere near Japan.

LOST GOLD OF JERUSALEM

IN THE LANGUEDOC REGION of southern France, high on a hilltop, is the isolated village named Rennes-le-Chateau. This is no ordinary village but one that lies at the heart of an extraordinary story about "the mystery of the priest's gold." The priest was Bérenger Saunèire who came to the village in 1885 as a young curate. He was also very poor. But by the time of his death in 1917, it is claimed that he had spent a fortune of up to $3.1 million. How he came by that fortune nobody knows for sure.

One of Sauniere's first jobs as priest was to raise money to restore the ancient church at Rennes-le-Chateau. It was more than 1,000 years old and the roof leaked and parts of the walls were collapsing. At the start of the restoration work, the church altar was being dismantled for repair. One of its carved stone legs was found to be hollow and inside were some ancient parchment scrolls. Two of these strange, old documents exist today and their discovery changed the life of the curate and started the legend of "the priest's gold."

Sauniere travelled to Paris with all the documents where he had them translated by experts. When he returned to his village he began spending large amounts of money. He bought a vast stretch of land beside the church where he proceeded to build an imposing villa with beautiful gardens. But where did all this new-found wealth come from? Sauniere's reply was always that he had been given some money by wealthy friends.

But how did the treasure come to a remote village in southern France? It had been captured when the Romans sacked Jerusalem in A.D. 70 and carried it back to Rome. Rome in turn was captured and sacked by a German tribe called the Visigoths in A.D. 410. They are supposed to have carried off the Temple treasure once again, this time to their lands in southern France. And this, people claim, was the source of Sauniere's incredible wealth, revealed to him in those ancient documents. The hunt for the priest's gold continues today.

THE FALL OF JERUSALEM

Ever since Jerusalem was captured by the Babylonians under King Nebuchadnezzar early in the sixth century B.C., the Jews had been ruled by other people. In A.D. 44 their state was made part of the Roman empire and there was a rebellion against Roman rule. In A.D. 70 Jerusalem was captured and the Temple was completely destroyed by fire.

◄ *Illumination from a 15th century manuscript showing the capture of Jerusalem by the Babylonians.*

▲ People have suggested that the lost treasure of Jerusalem of was brought to Rennes-le-Chateau by the Knights Templers after the crusader Wars.

▼ Stone carving from the Arch of Titus depicting Roman soldiers carrying off part of the gold from the Temple of Jerusalem. The Roman general Titus, later emperor, captured Jerusalem in A.D. 70.

▲ Bérenger Sauniere standing beside the hollow column fron the church altar. Many people believe the secret to his sudden riches had been hidden inside the column.

BLACKBEARD AND THE DEVIL

OF ALL THE PIRATES who prowled up and down the coasts of North America and the Caribbean islands in the 18th century, none was more feared than Edward "Blackbeard" Teach. Not only did he attack merchant ships and steal their cargoes, but he also raided the rich estates of plantation owners on the American mainland. Some of his favorite hunting grounds were the waters of the Carolinas.

Blackbeard's treasure

Blackbeard boasted that he had buried a huge amount of gold and silver treasure, in a place, "where none but Satan and myself can find it." Cruelty and boasting was quite normal among pirates, but Blackbeard was even feared and loathed by his fellow pirates because he stole from them as well. Blackbeard's years of terror and piracy came to an abrupt end off the coast of North Carolina in 1718 when he was shot dead by the British navy.

But what of the treasure he boasted about? He took the secret of its location to his grave, and so far the hoard has never been traced. Some people believe it may lie on Oak Island in Nova Scotia, but Blackbeard probably never traveled so far north. Others claim that he buried his loot on a beach on Plum Island off the New England coast. But if it did actually exist it will probably never be found.

➤ *Edward "Blackbeard" Teach in a picture made after his death in 1718. He is shown in a typically terrifying pose, with wild eyes and smoke pouring from the slow-burning fuses that he tied in his hair. He liked to drink a cocktail of rum and gunpowder*

Black Beard.　　Abdollah the Prince.

◀ *Blackbeard earned a reputation for treachery even among his fellow pirates. Many amazing stories were told about his bloodthirsty adventures. Here he is shown in a sword fight with Abdullah the Prince.*

UNITED
STATES OF
AMERICA

NOVA SCOTIA

VIRGINIA

NORTH CAROLINA

SOUTH CAROLINA

Black Beard's Island

Atlantic Ocean

CUBA

West Indies

Caribbean Sea

SOUTH AMERICA

▲ *Some people believe that Blackbeard's treasure may be buried on Blackbeard's island on the coast of South Carolinea*

WOMEN PIRATES

There were also women who took up piracy. Two of the most famous were Mary Read and Ann Bonny. Mary Read had been kidnapped by buccaneers in the early 18th century and joined them as a pirate. Ann Bonny was a privateer who attacked Spanish treasure ships. Both women dressed as men and were just as brave and terrifying as their fellow pirates

▶ *Mary Read was arrested for piracy in 1720 and died of fever in prison.*

CURSE OF THE THUNDER GOD

ON HIS DEATH BED in 1891, an eccentric gold prospector called Jake Walz whispered vague instructions about where a gold mine could be found.

It became known as the Old Dutchman mine after him. According to the story, Walz left California in about 1870 and moved across the border into Arizona. Soon after his arrival he started exploring the area around Superstition Mountain. One day he vanished among the canyons of the mountain and reappeared some time later clutching bags stuffed with gold nuggets. He said that he had found a seam of gold 18 inches (46 centimeters) wide running through the rock in one of the canyons.

But a curse lay on the gold and touched anyone who dared to steal it. The mountain lay in lands sacred to the Apache Native Americans and they were furious at this invasion of the home of their Thunder God. The young Apache girl who was thought to have led Walz to the gold had her tongue cut out. Walz returned to the mine and each time came away with more gold. He was followed by people keen to find out where the mine lay so his visits were usually made at night. He shot several men who tried to follow him and even murdered his own nephew because he was afraid his secret might get out. It seems that the Thunder God of the Apaches still stands guard over the forbidden secrets of the Old Dutchman mine.

▲ *Superstition Mountain lies in a desolate part of Phoenix, Arizona. It lies in lands that have been sacred to the Apache for generations.*

◄ *A portrait of John Sutter who owned the land in California where the 1848 great gold rush started.*

THE CALIFORNIA GOLD RUSH

Gold was first discovered in a river near Coloma, California in 1848 and within a year over 100,000 people had rushed into the state hoping to make their fortunes. Most of these "gold miners" had no knowledge of mining and many used spoons and knives with which to scratch away at the earth. Although many people did strike gold but there were far more who failed and who were left penniless and destitute.

▲ *A print published in 1849 showing people panning for gold during the gold rush.*

▲ *Many people died trying to find the gold in Superstition Mountain.*

▲ *The land of Arizona can be very dry and forbidding. Many people still believe that somewhere in one of the valleys surrounding Superstition Mountain a fortune in gold is waiting to be discovered.*

THE APACHE INDIANS

The Apaches are a tribe of Native Americans whose scattered lands once spread from western Arizona to central Texas and western Kansas. During the 19th century, they fought to keep their territory from the encroachments of the United States government and white settlers.

LOST GOLD FROM LITTLE BIG HORN

THE MOST SENSATIONAL battle in the drawn-out war between the Native Americans and the U.S. army took place on June 25, 1876. This was the Battle of the Little Big Horn. After years of seeing their land stolen by white settlers, the Native American tribes decided to fight back. The Sioux and the Cheyenne joined together, led by their chiefs Sitting Bull and Crazy Horse. Lieutenant-Colonel George Custer in command of a small U.S. force was to try and break the resistance of the Native Americans. But the U.S. government underestimated this threat and Custer's small unit of about two hundred men was completely wiped out by the much larger force of Sioux and Cheyenne warriors.

▲ *George Custer (1839-1876) shortly before he was killed at the Battle of Little Big Horn. He was a graduate of West Point military academy and fought in the Civil War.*

A forgotten fortune

Shortly after the battle, Captain Grant Marsh anchored his boat at the junction of the Big Horn and Little Horn rivers. The boat was carrying supplies for the U.S. army. As Marsh was keeping a look-out, two white men appeared with two covered carts. They begged Marsh to let them load their goods on to his boat. The "goods" turned out to be crates packed with $800,000 worth of gold bullion which the men were taking to Dakota. Marsh eventually agreed and the two travelers went on their way.

The next day, fighting in the area forced Marsh to sail down river. But before leaving, he buried the gold on the banks of the Big Horn river. Soon the captain and his boat were busy transporting wounded soldiers and the gold was left in its hiding place. Three years later Marsh tried to track down its rightful owners but with no success. In time the buried gold was forgotten and may still be lying somewhere beside the Big Horn river for, as far as is known, it was never collected.

➤ *A Sioux village, painted in the 1850s. Driven from their lands by white settlers, they tried to fight back. After the Battle of Little Big Horn the Sioux and Cheyenne were hunted down by U.S. troops and their villages destroyed.*

▲ *Some people suggest that treasure may be still be buried at the junction of the Big Horn and Little Horn rivers.*

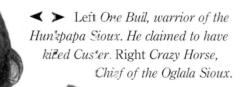

◄ ➤ Left *One Bull, warrior of the Hunkpapa Sioux. He claimed to have killed Custer. Right Crazy Horse, Chief of the Oglala Sioux.*

AFTER THE BATTLE OF LITTLE BIG HORN

Although it was the greatest victory for the Native Americans, it was to be their last. The Sioux and the Cheyenne were pursued by U.S. government troops and their villages destroyed. Starving and broken, they were forced to surrender. Their traditional homelands were taken away and they were forced to move to Reservations.

GLOSSARY

A

Aerial photography Photographs of the land taken from the air, either from an airplane or balloon. Aerial photographs can reveal signs of ancient towns, field boundaries, roads, tombs, and monuments, both above and below ground. Extreme weather, such as droughts or snow, often makes it easier to spot remains from the air than from the ground.

Aqualung The aqualung consists of air cylinders containing compressed air and a mouth-piece. A "demand regulator" feeds the diver with exactly the amount of air needed. This invention opened up a new period of underwater exploration. The aqualung was invented in 1943 by two Frenchmen, Jacques Cousteau and Emile Gagnan.

Archeologist The word archeology means "the study of everything ancient." Archeology is about building up a picture of how people lived in the past from the clues they have left behind. Archeologists work like detectives, gathering evidence and suggesting theories to explain their discoveries.

Aristocracy This literally means government by the best citizens, from the Greek word *aristokratia* meaning rule by the best born. Today an aristocracy is the high born, privileged or noble class of a country.

Armada A large number of ships (or airplanes). From the Latin word *armare* meaning to provide with arms. The Spanish Armada was the great fleet of ships sent by King Philip II of Spain against England in 1588.

Artefact Something made or shaped by a person, such as a tool or work of art, especially an archeological object.

Aztecs A warrior people who established a vast empire centered on the valley of Mexico. It was very well organized with beautiful cities, a complex religion and laws. It was overthrown in 1519 by Hernan Cortes and his followers of Spanish conquistadors.

B

Bitumen A thick, black, sticky liquid that can become very hard when exposed to the air. It is a mixture of petroleum, natural gas and a substance called asphalt. In ancient times it was used as a kind of mortar and the ancient Egyptians used it in the preparation of mummies. Today it is used for road surfacing and roofing.

Booty Any valuable article or articles, especially when stolen.

Bronze A yellow or brown metal made by mixing copper and tin. It is harder than copper and also resists corrosion. It was used a lot by early people during the period of history known as the Bronze Age (dating about 5000-1200 B.C. in the Middle East and about 2000-500 B.C. in Europe).

Buccaneer A member of various groups of seafarers who robbed Spanish ships and colonies on the Spanish American coast during the 17th century. They were not true pirates as they were commissioned to rob by a government or some other authority.

Bullion Gold and silver in the form of bars and ingots. Bullion was transported in huge "treasure ships" from South America to Europe where it was melted down to make coins, jewelry and works of art.

C

Cameo A small carving with a raised surface made from semi-precious stones, shells or glass. A pale-colored surface layer is carved to show a darker ground. Fine cameos were produced in ancient Greece and Rome, during the Renaissance, and in the Victorian era. They were used for decorating cups and vases and in pieces of jewelry.

Carbon 14 dating A technique for calculating the age of organic materials. Living things, like plants and animals, contain something called Carbon 14. When they die, the amount of Carbon 14 in them gets less. Experts can measure the amount of it in the object they are examining and then calculate its age.

Casket A small box or chest for valuables, especially for jewels or gold.

Cenote A natural well or reservoir. In the ancient Yucatan, cenotes were places of religious worship.

Characteristic A distinguishing quality, attribute or trait.

Coffer A chest, often wooden, for storing clothes or valuables. Usually larger than a casket.

Conquistador The Spanish word for conqueror. The term refers to the Spanish soldiers and adventurers who conquered Central and South America in the 16th century.

Conservation The preservation and careful management of an object, building or landscape. It is very important to preserve ancient objects once they have been excavated so that they do not decay any further.

Cremate To burn up something, especially a body, and reduce it to ash. The custom of cremation was common among the ancient Greeks and Romans, but was discontinued among Christians until the late 19th century because of their belief in the bodily resurrection of the dead.

Crusades Military expeditions launched in the 11th-

13th centuries by the Christian powers of Europe to capture the Holy Lands from the Muslims. The word comes from the Latin word *crux* meaning cross.

Curate A clergyman who is in charge of a parish or who has been appointed to assist a parish priest.

D

Diadem A circlet of gold or some other precious metal, or a light, jeweled crown indicating royal power.

Dissolution of the Monasteries From 1534-1539, monasteries in England were closed and sold on the pretext of immorality and other abuses. This followed King Henry VIII's break with the Roman Catholic Church and the formation of the Anglican (English Protestant) Church.

Dynasty A sequence or family of hereditary rulers.

E

Ewer A large jug or pitcher with a wide mouth.

F

French Revolution The period 1789-1799 that saw the end of the French monarchy and the establishment of the First Republic. The nobility were stripped of their lands and titles and King Louis XVI was executed in 1793.

Founder To founder (of a ship etc.) is to sink in water or become stuck in soft ground.

G

Garnet A hard, glassy, deep red gemstone. Many of the gold treasures found in the Sutton Hoo ship burial were
decorated with cut and polished garnets.

Governor A person who governs a province or a foreign colony on behalf of the ruling government.

Griffin A mythical winged monster with the head, forelegs and wings of an eagle, and the body, tail and hind- legs of a lion. It was believed to be the guardian of hidden treasure.

H

Hieroglyphs A form of writing, especially as used in ancient Egypt, in which pictures or symbols are used to represent objects, ideas or sounds. Each hieroglyph corresponded to the sound of one or more letters. At the same time, a symbol could also represent an object.

Hippodrome In ancient Greece and in the Roman empire, this was an open-air course for horse and chariot races. It had a long, rectangular shape with rounded ends. The horses raced down the length of one side of the course, turned at the end and then raced up the other side.

Hold The space in a ship or airplane, usually below the decks, for storing cargo.

Holy Sepulcher, Church of the The church which was built over the tomb (The Holy Sepulcher) in Jerusalem in which the body of Christ was laid after the Crucifixion. The first church on the site was built in A.D. 335 by Constantine, the first Christian Roman emperor.

I

Icon A picture of Christ, the Virgin Mary or a saint, especially one painted in oils on a wooden panel. Icons are particularly venerated in the Eastern Church. They are sometimes portable, in the form of small folding panels.

Incas The ancient rulers of Peru. From the 13th century until their destruction in the 15th century, their territory extended from what is now Chile, through Peru into Ecuador. Their empire was destroyed in 1532 by the Spanish conquistador Francisco Pizarro.

Ingot A piece of cast metal – often gold, silver or copper – in the shape of a small brick made in a mould. This shape is easy to transport and is then melted down for use.

L

Lacquer A varnish used to give a hard, shiny finishing surface to wood, metal and stone. Chinese and Japanese lacquers are obtained from the resin of a tree called *Rhus vernicifera*.

Loot Goods stolen during war or riots, or any goods, money or treasure obtained illegally.

M

Mesopotamia From the Greek word meaning between the rivers. It was the region between the Euphrates and Tigris rivers, now the country of Iraq. It was the cradle of the Sumerian civilization and of the empires of Babylon and Assyria.

Muslim A follower of the religion of Islam. Islam was first proclaimed in about 610 by Mohammed, Prophet of the one God (Allah).

N

Necropolis A burial site or cemetery. From the Greek word *nekros*, meaning dead body, and *polis*, meaning city.

Nomad A member of a people or tribe who move from place to place to find pasture for their animals and food for themselves.

O

Organic A living thing, such as a plant, animal or human.

P

Pagan Someone who worships a number of different gods.

Parchment The skin of certain animals, such as sheep and goats, used as a writing surface. Once it has been treated and dried, the skin is polished smooth.

Perishable Something that is liable to rot and decay.

Pharaoh A king of ancient Egypt. The word comes from the Egyptian title *per-'o* which means Great House.

Platinum A heavy, grey-white precious metal, harder than silver, which does not corrode. It is used in jewelry and for industrial purposes.

Plunder To steal valuables from a city or religious building, especially in times of war.

Porcelain A fine, hard chinaware made from kaolin clay. The process of making porcelain was invented by the Chinese during the T'ang dynasty (618-907).

Portico A type of porch or entrance to a building, consisting of a roof supported by columns.

Praxiteles A Greek sculptor who flourished in 360-340 B.C. and whose work is regarded as among the finest ever made.

Q
Quest The search for something.

R
Regalia Ceremonial emblems (such as crown, orb and scepter), and robes of royalty or some high position.

Relic Something that has survived from the past, such as an object or custom. In religion, a relic is part of the body of a saint or something used by or associated with a saint and venerated as holy.

S
Saladin In Arabic *Salah-ed-Din*, the great Sultan of Syria and Egypt who lived in about 1137-1193. He led the Muslim armies which swept the crusaders out of Jerusalem and much of the Holy Land.

Salamander An amphibian with four legs and a tail. Although it looks like a lizard it is not the same as it has no scales or claws but a smooth, moist skin. In old stories, the mythical salamander was supposed to live in fire and became a symbol of everlasting life.

Salvage The process of rescuing ships or their cargoes from loss at sea.

Satellite photography Aerial photography taken from satellites. Like aerial photography, this technique can show up ancient remains that are invisible on the ground.

Scroll A roll of parchment or paper, usually with writing on it. Ancient books and official records were often in the form of scrolls.

Shrine A place of religious worship associated with a holy person or relic. Famous shrines include the tomb of St Peter in Rome and the Buddhist Temple of the Tooth in Kandy, Sri Lanka.

Silt A fine deposit of mud, clay or sand, especially in a river or lake.

Sovereign A person who exercises absolute authority. The ruler, especially a king or queen, of a country.

Soviet Relating to the Soviet Union, the U.S.S.R. – Union of Soviet Socialist Republics. There were fifteen union republics with the main, central government based in Moscow. The union broke up in 1991.

T
Topaz A hard, glassy yellow gemstone.

Tsar
The imperial title for the emperor of Russia. It derives from the Latin word *caesar*.

Tyrol Or Tirol. A province of Austria, near the border with Italy.

V
Vaulted A vaulted roof is an arched roof. The roof of teh Vergina tomb is one of the earliest examples of a true vault found in the Greek world.

X
X-ray A form of electromagnetic radiation. X-rays were first identified in 1895 by a German scientist called Wilhelm Rontgen.

Z
Ziggurat A step pyramid. In ancient Assyria and Babylonia it was made of sun-baked bricks faced with glazed bricks or tiles. On top stood a shrine to a god. The most famous ziggurat is the Tower of Babel mentioned in the Bible.

Index